Teachers and Young Researchers in Action

With an increasing emphasis on the role of evidence in education, primary school teachers need to find meaningful ways to engage in research. *Teachers and Young Researchers in Action* supports teachers and children in carrying out meaningful classroom research that can transform practice. An accessible guide, it shows the different ways in which children and teachers can go about their research, the problems they may meet on the way and the tried and tested methods to meet those challenges.

Illustrated with rich real-life examples of research projects – exploring rewards and sanctions, values education, school structures and reading for pleasure – it shows how we can celebrate the importance of the voice of the child in school life, benefitting individual children, teachers and schools alike. This accessible book outlines the benefits of children's research for individual children, teachers and schools as well as providing case studies that demonstrate how young children's research projects can be successful.

Written for teachers by teachers, this go-to resource will be of interest to anyone working with children as researchers looking to improve their practice and in need of guidance and support.

Viv Randall, in her role as executive headteacher, was committed and dedicated to developing the capabilities and potential of young children to act as informed voices in the cycle of school improvement. Their development as young researchers proved a crucial feature in effective self-evaluation.

Debbie Reel, lecturer in childhood studies and education, has spent her 27-year career teaching both in primary and higher education. Her educational background in learning and teaching has fuelled her goal of ensuring that we all, through action research, contribute within the educational arena and that here, children's voices are both included and valued.

Nicola Smith worked in primary schools in Worcestershire and Birmingham before becoming an adult education tutor and then a lecturer in childhood studies and ITE. She has been involved in the Young Researchers Project for six years and is particularly interested in how the youngest children in school can be researchers.

Teachers and Young Researchers in Action

Working Together to Transform Practice

Viv Randall, Debbie Reel and Nicola Smith

Routledge
Taylor & Francis Group

LONDON AND NEW YORK

First published 2021
by Routledge
2 Park Square, Milton Park, Abingdon, Oxon OX14 4RN

and by Routledge
52 Vanderbilt Avenue, New York, NY 10017

Routledge is an imprint of the Taylor & Francis Group, an informa business

British Library Cataloguing-in-Publication Data
A catalogue record for this book is available from the British Library

Library of Congress Cataloging-in-Publication Data

Names: Randall, Viv, author. | Reel, Debbie, author. | Smith, Nicola (Lecturer in childhood studies), author.
Title: Teachers and young researchers in action : working together to transform practice / Viv Randall, Debbie Reel, and Nicola Smith.
Description: Abingdon, Oxon; New York, NY : Routledge, 2021. | Includes bibliographical references and index.
Identifiers: LCCN 2020038749 | ISBN 9780367144418 (hardback) | ISBN 9780367144425 (paperback) | ISBN 9780429032035 (ebook)
Subjects: LCSH: Action research in education. | Research--Methodology--Study and teaching (Elementary)--Great Britain. | Teacher-student relationships--Great Britain.
Classification: LCC LB1028.24 .R36 2021 | DDC 370.21--dc23
LC record available at https://lccn.loc.gov/2020038749

ISBN: 978-0-367-14441-8 (hbk)
ISBN: 978-0-367-14442-5 (pbk)
ISBN: 978-0-429-03203-5 (ebk)

Typeset in Bembo
by SPi Global, India

This book is dedicated to all our inspirational young researchers, with thanks to Professor Jean McNiff for encouraging us to start writing.

Contents

Chapter One

Introducing the Young Researchers Project

Viv Randall, Debbie Reel and Nicola Smith

Introduction

In this chapter, we introduce you to the Young Researchers Project and our role in it. We explain the purpose of this book and provide a brief summary of the content of each chapter.

Encouraging young children to engage in research has always been a topic we have championed in our roles as teachers, teacher educators and heads of schools. Each of us, within our own professional remit, has read about, researched and observed children as researchers. We have attended and presented at conferences and listened to the voices of children, who have a right to influence the educational arena in which they are situated. The experiences that we share, although different, have united us in being able to write this book. We remain indebted to researchers such as Mary Kellett and Sue Bucknall, whose research on children as researchers has influenced us strongly. To begin with, it was Viv's determination to raise expectations and aspirations of the very young and those who teach them, as well as seeking partnerships with a local university, that brought us together. After five years of working together, we decided that we wanted to share the work that the teachers and children of the Young Researchers Project are doing and so began to write this book.

The Young Researchers Project involves around ten primary and secondary schools in Birmingham every year. Small groups of children (usually six to eight) work on a research project of their choosing, supported by one of their teachers. The projects begin in November and end in May/June. Towards the beginning of the project, we meet with the young researchers at our University Day, to talk to them about how to carry out the research. Throughout the year, there are regular meetings between children and adults involved in the projects to discuss progress. At the end of the year, children present their research findings at the Young Researchers Conference, held at University College Birmingham.

Working each year with young researchers towards an annual conference and the various experiences and challenges we have faced has provided us with a strong foundation on which to write the book. Our experiences of working with different, talented and inspirational young researchers have always left us on a high note, wanting and willing to share our experiences with others. Having the time to share this experience has always been an issue; however, we knew the importance of making the time to share our knowledge of promoting ways in which teachers can engage young researchers in making a difference within schools and communities. It was also important to us that, in the writing of this book, teachers were given the opportunity to share their experiences of this research process. Their accounts of the Young Researchers Project provide a real-life sense of what is involved, supporting other teachers who might want to engage children as researchers. This has probably been our greatest challenge; pulling together ideas and experiences from different teachers, in different schools teaching different ages and groups of children. However, we felt that hearing the voices of those teachers' experiences was essential to this publication, and we are grateful for all the work that they have contributed to the project.

Our joint involvement in the Young Researchers Project has gone on for five years now and the project continues to flourish. For four of those five years, we have discussed the reality of writing this book, and just over a year in the making, we are now here and we hope that this fuels your ability to start a Young Researchers Project of your own. Although this book contains some templates and writing about how to carry out your own project, it is not a 'How to' book. Working with young researchers will 'look' different in different contexts and you will need to develop your own ways of working on projects. This book is designed to help you reflect on the issues that may encounter as you embark on your own Young Researchers Project, with real-life examples of teachers and children who have done just this.

Structure of the book

Chapter 2 is written by Viv Randall, whose early work with young researchers in Birmingham is the foundation of the Young Researchers Project. This chapter explains how her work with children as researchers began. In particular, it focuses on the contribution of young researchers to school improvement.

Chapter 3 is written by Nicola Smith and Debbie Reel, who support the Young Researchers Project in their role as university academics. It explains our view of children as competent and capable researchers, able to examine issues of relevance in their own lives, schools and communities. It also considers some of the issues related to children's voice and participation that we have encountered in the project.

Chapter 4 is also written by Debbie Reel and Nicola Smith. It explores how universities and schools work together on the Young Researchers Project. It includes some consideration of key events in the project: the University Day and the Young Researchers Conference.

Chapters 5 to 8 are case studies of Young Researchers Projects in primary and secondary schools in Birmingham. The case studies are written by four teachers who have been involved in the Young Researchers Project: Kerry Orme, Tara Harris, Paul Clabon and Steven Moore. Each case study is followed by a commentary written by Debbie Reel and Nicola Smith, linking back to the notions of children's voice and participation discussed in Chapter 3.

Chapter 9 is written by Debbie Reel and Nicola Smith. It contains some guidance and templates to support teachers who want to begin working on their own Young Researchers Project. Links to other useful publications are also provided.

Chapter 10 is written with Debbie Reel by Ali Fisher, the Teaching School Manager who is responsible for managing the day-to-day running of the Young Researchers Project, keeping us all on track and well organised. In this chapter, Ali and Debbie consider how the project might develop in the future.

Chapter Two

The Young Researchers Project

Viv Randall

Introduction

This chapter outlines the beginnings of the Young Researchers Project in Birmingham. It explains how the project began and how it has developed over the last 14 years. In particular, it focuses on how the Young Researchers Project has made a meaningful contribution to school improvement across the city.

The beginnings of the Young Researchers Project

The Young Researchers Project began in the school where I was headteacher, Colmore Infant and Nursery School in Birmingham. The journey to become a school where very young children could have an active and dynamic voice around school improvement began in 2003, when I was assigned the role of Primary Strategy Consultant Leader by the National College. This role involved supporting and challenging leaders at all levels to improve standards and outcomes in their school. In return, Primary Strategy Consultant Leaders were given opportunities to network and develop their own skill set and thinking through a programme of training and development opportunities. As a result, in 2003 Colmore Infant and Nursery School was nominated by the Local Authority to work with the NFER (National Federation of Educational Research) on a two-year research project, investigating the 'Research Engaged School' (Sharp et al., 2005). Handscombe and MacBeath (2003) suggested that schools could become 'research engaged' if research and enquiry were placed at the centre of school improvement. The NFER team set out to further explore this idea with 15 primary and secondary schools across the country, of which three were in Birmingham, including my own school. The driving force behind the initiative came from the premise that education policy was changing at a brisk and radical pace and with a focus on accurate self-evaluation for OFSTED, the use of action-based research could provide informed, considered evidence, which was seen to be highly effective (Mukherji & Albon, 2010).

The school was paired with a researcher from the NFER, Dr Dawn Sanders, who provided support and challenge to the teacher researchers involved. The project, which took place over the next year, was published by the NFER in 2005 but the legacy of reflection and enquiry continued (Sharp et al., 2005). The impact of the research was to create a culture of continuous development for all at Colmore School with significant emphasis placed on linking the research findings to the school improvement plan. However, I knew that we were missing something, namely a consideration of the voices of children as being at the centre of our work in school.

All staff were viewed as researchers at the school, either in an active or passive role, but the voice of the child was not a key feature. Reading Kellett's (2005) publication focussing on developing children as researchers led me to the realisation that the ability and potential of young children to carry out meaningful research was being overlooked. It was at this point that I decided to investigate whether I could challenge the assumption that children as young as five years old were not capable of carrying out meaningful research work that could impact on school outcomes and provision.

A group of highly confident and high-attaining Year 1 pupils were chosen to research an identified area for improvement, which was proving to be hard to shift. The research question chosen was, 'How do we know if children are learning in the outdoor classroom?' This question was selected because monitoring showed that staff in early years did not use the outdoor environment as part of children's learning experiences. Activities or experiences were not planned and both teachers and teacher assistants, first, did not want to go outside and, second, were unsure about what to do when they did. The issue of involving high-attaining children is something discussed in Chapter 4, but for the purpose of this research, this group of children were the focus. When we began the research, school staff were reluctant to change, and any training to date on children as researchers had proved ineffective and with no impact. This dilemma helped to shape the question for the first research project and knowing how beneficial the challenge of a 'real' researcher had been to teachers' research work, NFER researchers were asked to support the same challenge and level of questioning that they had previously provided. Dr Dawn Saunders and Dr Caroline Sharpe both acted as critical friends to the group and encouraged and challenged them to think through the research process and gain understanding from it. The project was innovative and thought provoking for adults as the children suggested insightful and heartfelt solutions to the research question. These young researchers were able to show, through their information gathering and discussion with their peers, just how much enjoyment and increased levels of concentration and resilience the pupils were able to demonstrate when learning outdoors. However, the young researchers struggled with the question of how to find out how much the pupils had learnt outdoors. As one perceptive young researcher stated, 'How can we find out when we can't see what's inside their heads?' Dawn supported the children with forming the kind of questions that would help them to discover what had been learnt from a simple yet creative maths activity outside. The results helped them to hypothesise that, for the majority of pupils, their learning had been made far more explicit with the use of concrete and practical problems to solve. This also was a revelation to the staff team when the researchers presented them with their research project and findings. As the children felt nervous about presenting to an audience, it was decided that they should record their findings on a film, which was shown to staff, governors and parents. This was probably one of the most successful change management activities we had ever undertaken. The impact went beyond making changes to practice in terms of the use of the outdoors, as the project also dramatically changed staff perceptions of the value of the child's voice and the depth of their understanding.

As a result, the NFER asked Graham Handscombe to review the work and the film was shared with universities both in the UK and internationally, showing, first, that with support the research process can be followed and understood by such young children and, second, that the child's voice is a powerful tool for change (Clark & Moss, 2011, Mukherji & Albon, 2010). The next stage was to spread the practice at Colmore Infant and Nursery School and to other local schools, through the school's involvement with a Network Learning Community (Kerr et al., 2003). I was given the responsibility of developing the research and development arm of the brief. Consequently in 2005 the first Children as Researchers conference was born involving eight local schools with their individual projects. The conference gave the opportunity for children to describe in detail their research journey to each other, which was a new experience for all of them. They were used to explaining their learning to fellow classmates and teachers at their own schools but to do this to a wide and varied audience of unfamiliar adults and pupils from a range of ages and settings was entirely unfamiliar.

Children were used to adults being seen as the 'experts' and therefore providing all of the answers, so to have their outcomes potentially being used to influence and change practice was an exciting prospect. As Bucknall (2012, p. 19) states 'A crucial factor in the development of children's competence might be adults' confidence in this ability'. In addition, equal weighting was given to the findings and hypotheses of each research group so that all participants, regardless of their age, felt both confident enough to explain and justify their own work as well as cross examine the findings of others. It was important that as part of the ongoing support process for the lead research teachers, a commonality of language and expectations were shared. This ensured that all of the projects followed set guidelines, which allowed all of the pupils to both understand the research process and be able to answer questions that arose, regardless of their age or experience. Consequently, at the conferences, the young researchers would independently ask questions of another school's methods and findings and then use the responses to inform their own next steps. Equally, teachers who listened to the questions would frequently follow them up with communication to another school about how they might use the results of the research in their own schools. This was particularly evident in questions around the use of marking, reward systems and the impact of curriculum changes. This powerful and insightful dialogue was and continues to be a revelation, particularly to the adults involved. The age of children as active researchers in Birmingham was launched.

It was felt to be really important that the children's research conference be organised in the same way as any adult conference; with high-profile keynote speakers, individual presentations and a discussion forum. In this way the expectations for performance, participation and outcomes were raised for all parties and we were not disappointed.

However, in this first tranche of research work with children, several aspects could have been improved and as a result lessons were learnt. At first, there was an assumption that all teachers would understand the research cycle itself after a short training session and would be able to effectively guide their research group through the steps with clarity and knowledge. In reality, in some cases teachers struggled to do this. The continuing challenge that not all teachers were able to attend progress meetings to share the process and seek advice and support added to the variability of outcomes and the quality of what could be viewed as, 'thorough research methods' (Waller & Bitou, 2011). In considering these issues of variability and quality, the involvement and commitment of the headteachers was a significant factor. Successful projects took place in schools where research as a recognised method of influencing school improvement was integral to whole school practice. As stated by Cheeseman and Walker (2019, p.61), 'To lead others is to empower people to think both independently and collectively'. The active involvement of the headteachers first raised the status of the work and, second, ensured that the teachers, who were leading on the work, were well supported and enabled to carry out the work with dedicated time allocated and protected. This has remained a key feature in shaping the success of the current Young Researchers Project.

The Young Researchers Project and school improvement

In 2006, I became a National Leader in Education along with the headteacher of our partner school, Colmore Juniors. Together, we worked with schools who, following their OFSTED inspections, had gone into Special Measures. The improvement work in the form of school to school support helped to not only sharpen and improve our own practice but to reinforce the significance and educational benefits of encouraging children to become an integral part of that work. After systems, staffing and processes had been established, we raised the question as to whether these supported schools could develop their own pupils as researchers and see what the benefits might be and if not, what was stopping them? The schools felt that they could take on their research work when they were nearing the end of their journey out of special measures as staffing would be more stable and the quality of teaching and learning improved. They then felt able and more confident to re-focus on what the impact of pupil research could have on whole school improvement. It was heartwarming to see schools who had once struggled to manage on a day-to-day basis emerge as some of the most passionate and dedicated young researchers schools. They could see and value how a child's voice and perspective added a depth and quality to their improvement work and embraced it fully. One of the schools' latest OFSTED report (2017) stated:

> Pupils describe the school's curriculum as 'inspiring'. They spoke animatedly to inspectors about the rich experiences they have. Leaders ensure that pupils have opportunities to excel in many ways. For example, all pupils learn at least one musical instrument and have the chance to perform in public. The curriculum explicitly promotes pupils' problem-solving and research skills.

The Colmore schools were designated as a National Teaching School in 2013 and named Colmore Partnership Teaching Schools Alliance (CPTSA). At least 20 local good and outstanding schools joined the alliance, not only to gain support but to access training and development opportunities. As part of the role of every TSA, research was identified as a key work strand. However, in many cases, this was the least popular area and often avoided. The need to enhance and strengthen teachers' engagement with meaningful research is deemed as highly important (Wells, 2014), therefore developing children as researchers became a priority for the schools in the CPTSA. The research strand of the alliance grew and became exciting, innovative and entirely relevant, resulting in this strand becoming the most popular for staff involvement. It also provided a gateway for pupils and staff across the alliance to work and learn together and showcase the findings at an annual conference. The previous inspection at Colmore Infant school also helped to motivate the schools' interests to take on research in a far more proactive way than they might have done previously. An extract of the report below was helpful in influencing the alliance schools to become enthusiastically involved and to provide us with access to a group of schools with shared values and commitment.

> Academic learning is not restricted to the classroom. Pupils have undertaken research into what helps them learn and presented the findings to national conferences. They have surveyed the local community to identify any concerns they may have and then worked with the police to resolve parking issues. Such activities effectively support pupils' contribution to the community. Their achievements are a shining example of what pupils of such a young age can do, and leave them exceptionally well prepared for the next stage of their education.
>
> (OFSTED October 2011, Colmore Infant & Nursery School)

University partnership

As the work developed and became more refined, it was decided to give the research questions a greater focus so that direct links to individual school improvement plans could be seen and the impact of the research work monitored and reported upon. This avoided the 'show and tell' approach that had been observed, particularly from schools that were new to the project, understandably as they, again, had not had the rigour or challenge and support through this process. Despite this, the themes had begun to show a far deeper alignment to whole school issues and wider areas for improvement. Elevating children's work from school project presentations to meaningful, quality research work has been the driving force behind the evolution of developing young researchers. It was very difficult initially to try and persuade teachers to understand the potential capabilities and independence of young children and to dissuade them from directing the outcomes too much. For some teachers, to begin with the research work was interpreted as showcasing a class project, for example on local history topics, rather than using it to examine an area of concern in school improvement terms. It was with much hand holding, coaching and challenging questioning that teachers were led to a world where children's views, supported by their in-depth research, highlighted areas for improvement that challenge teachers' and leaders' thinking and practice. It took a great deal of confidence both from the lead teachers and their senior teams to allow children to lead curriculum improvements even if that meant teachers having to change their own practice.

What had made the research work with young people successful initially was the challenge and support provided by an academic researcher. It provided rigour and substance to the projects and ensured that pupils (and teachers) engaged in age appropriate research principles and guidelines. This, in turn, gave the projects credibility, an absolutely vital element if pupils' work was to be taken seriously and then used effectively by staff in schools to impact on outcomes or provision. So it was a teaching school partnership with University College Birmingham (UCB) that offered to provide this crucial missing element. From 2015, UCB not only hosted the conferences but provided a university experience for the children, the University Day, as discussed in more detail in Chapters 4 and 9. This included a lecture on the research process, skilfully put into accessible child-friendly language. Within this session, aspects covering question design, differences between qualitative and quantitative research, effective research methods and ethics are all covered along with and an opportunity to visit the university campus raising aspirations seeing how students learnt there. The session demonstrated effectively to the children how to carry out their research without bias or prejudice, which was reflected in the results.

In addition, Debbie Reel and Nicola Smith have acted as research assistants to each school supporting children as they provide digests for some of the research already published within their chosen area. The aim here is for children to be able to access academic research and findings on their theme and to have the opportunity to ask further questions that arise as their research journey progressed. The expectation is that this academic element will then form part of the children's research project, informing and providing either an opposing or sympathetic view whilst teaching children an important element of the research process. Some of the research subjects covered to date include reward systems, school partnerships, usefulness of homework, human rights, well-being, teaching methods and the impact of the use of technology. Results are presented as PowerPoint presentations or, since 2018, in poster form. Every poster and accompanying hand-out is structured to show full academic investigations; each with the research question, context, rationale, methodology, findings and reflections. Each school is then quizzed and questioned about their findings by their fellow researchers and children explain their work with clarity and enthusiasm.

High-profile keynote speakers have included Jean McNiff, Professor of Educational Research at York St John University; Professor Danielle Carey, former Dean of UCB's School of Education; Professor Peter Kraftl, Dr Sophie Hadfield-Hall and Ruth Till of the University of Birmingham; and Tim Boyes, CEO of Birmingham Education Partnership. All of these eminent speakers have added the weight, gravitas and credibility to the Young Researchers Project work that has been so important in our drive to show that not only do young children have massive untapped potential but also a huge amount of influence to change and impact on school improvement.

Developing children as researchers has been the most exciting and empowering part of my work as a headteacher. It has really shown me the importance of the child's voice in the life of a school not only through discussion but now in a well-considered, structured and thought provoking way that impacts directly on school improvement.

References

Cheeseman, S. & Walker, R. (2019) *Pedagogies for Leading Practice*. Routledge: Abingdon.

Clark, A. & Moss, P. (2011) *Listening to Young Children: The Mosaic Approach* (2nd edition). NCB: London.

Bucknall, S. (2012) *Children as Researchers in Primary Schools*. Routledge: Oxon.

Handscombe, G. & MacBeath, J. (2003) *The Research-engaged School*. Essex County Council: Chelmsford.

Kellet, M. (2005) *How to Develop Children as Researchers: A Step By Step Guide to Teaching the Research Process*. Paul Chapman Publishing: London.

Kerr, D., Aiston, S., White, K., Holland, M. & Grayson, H. (2003) *Literature Review of Networked Learning Communities*. NFER: Slough.

Mukherji, P. & Albon, D. (2010) *Research Methods in Early Childhood: An Introductory Guide*. Sage: London.

Sharp, C., Eames, A., Sanders, D. & Tomlinson, K. (2005) *Postcards from Research-engaged Schools*. NFER: Slough.

Waller, T. & Bitou, A. (2011) Research *with* children: Three challenges for participatory research in early childhood. *European Early Childhood Education Research Journal* Vol 19, No 1, pp 5–20.

Wells, M. (2014) Elements of professional sustainable leaning. *Professional Development in Education* Vol 5, No 3, pp 488–504.

Chapter Three

Young researchers

Nicola Smith and Debbie Reel

Introduction

This chapter will explore the idea of children as competent, capable researchers and how this influences the relationships between adults and children involved in the Young Researchers Project. In particular, it will examine how we ensure that adults support children to be listened to and heard in the project. It considers the notion of children's 'voice' in relation to working with children as researchers, including the importance of inclusion. We go on to consider principles of participation and how these underpin the work of the Young Researchers Project. At the end of this chapter, we highlight some of the successes of the Young Researchers Project to date; namely the involvement of children as young as five; continued participation in the project over several years; the development of key skills and attributes in our young researchers and the widening influence of school-based research projects.

Relationships and the child as a researcher

Working with children as researchers raises several questions around relationships, with a particular issue in relation to power dynamics. Previous projects involving child researchers have wrestled with the challenges involved in the imbalance of power between adults and children in a research context (e.g. Bucknall, 2010; Murray, 2014). Bucknall (2010) points out that such power imbalances are particularly problematic in the context of schools, where children and teachers have existing relationships that, to differing extents, rely on teachers making decisions that impact directly on the lives of children. Furthermore, teachers do not necessarily involve the children in this decision-making process. If we were to see research as a field in which we, as teachers and academics, are the 'experts' and children are the 'novices', then the Young Researchers Project would be likely to reinforce the existing power dynamic, arguably with the result that children were not acting as true researchers in the project.

However, our view of research is that we are all developing our capabilities in, and understanding of, the research process. As Kamler and Thomson (2008) assert in their writing on the experiences of PhD students, carrying out research is a process of "becoming and belonging" part of the established research community. Thus everyone involved in the Young Researchers Project is on this journey of "becoming and belonging"; academics, teachers and children. As academics, being part of the project has challenged us to think about the meaning and motivation of educational research. We have also had to carefully consider our thinking on methodology; for example, in order to explain ethics in research to children, we have had to be very clear about our own beliefs and approaches in relation to ethics. The work of Clark and Moss (2011) and Murray (2014) demonstrates that children engage in research behaviours naturally and are active enquirers in their own social worlds. Furthermore, Bradbury-Jones and Taylor (2015) refer to young researchers as a, "powerful conduit for other children's voices." (p. 161). Thus our role on the Young Researchers Project is to support children in developing their competence as researchers and to scaffold their involvement in the research projects (Bucknall, 2010).

As adults supporting and scaffolding children's research projects, we are mindful of existing power dynamics as well as the difficulties inherent in considering the notion of children's 'voice' in schools. Several researchers (e.g. Kellett, 2005; Pascal & Bertram, 2014; Bucknall, 2010) have highlighted the importance of hearing the voice of the child in research and this notion has gained credence in Birmingham schools since the introduction of initiatives designed to fulfil the requirements of the United Nations Convention on the Rights of the Child (United Nations, 1989). Previous experiences in our own research projects had highlighted the importance of child voice in relation to school life (Smith, 2014). However, there is a danger that in seeing the Young Researchers Project as a means of 'giving' children voice, the project itself could reinforce the existing imbalance of power between adult and child participants. Here we find Kay Haw's (1996, p. 321) notion useful; she sees research as being something that might, "Open up spaces for the 'voices' [of participants] in places where they would not normally be heard". Thus like Fraser et al. (2004) we intend the Young Researchers Project to develop a 'discursive space' where children's voice may be heard, rather than to be an opportunity for adults to 'give' children voice from a position of power.

Our work on the Young Researchers Project is based on a view of children as competent and social beings, who are co-constructors of their own knowledge and understanding (Lyndon et al., 2019). This means that we see children as capable of forming their own research questions, making research methodology decisions, collecting and analysing data and interpreting their own findings. However, we also assert that, rather than children being seen as separate from adults in terms of competencies, both adults and children are context-dependent beings. Although children have agency, their ability to enact this agency is related to the opportunities afforded to them to do so. This means that if we are going to expect children to design their own research projects then we need to make sure that the opportunities for them to do so are provided, and more importantly that this work is carefully supported and scaffolded. This support and scaffolding begins with the University Day and continues throughout the project, as explored in more detail in Chapter 4 and in the case study chapters later in this book.

It is important to consider that not everyone might see the benefit of allowing children to be seen as powerful or worthy of being listened to in the context of school. However, we would argue that in the current research context, it is important that children are involved as active participants in researching and shaping their own school lives. The current emphasis on evidence-based practice has highlighted the importance of teachers situating their classroom strategies on an understanding of 'what works' (Biesta, 2007). However, as Wiliams (2018) points out, "Everything works somewhere, nothing works everywhere". Children are in the unique position of being able to shine a light on their own learning lives in a way that can help teachers to understand what works for them and their peers and why, in the contexts in which they find themselves (Clark & Moss, 2011; Brooker, 2002).

Developing a more inclusive approach

Working with children as researchers requires us to build on the significant body of knowledge that exists around listening to children (Clark, 2017). As a discursive space, the Young Researchers Project opens up a space where children's voices can be heard by adults, but also where they can seek out and listen to the voices of their peers. We have a responsibility here to ensure that, in doing so, we adopt an inclusive approach, so that it is not just certain groups of children who are being listened to. The case study below demonstrates how Taylor, a primary school teacher in Birmingham, developed a more inclusive approach to carrying out projects with young researchers in her own school.

Developing a more inclusive approach: Case Study

Taylor has been involved as a teacher with the Young Researchers Project for several years. For her most recent project, she was interested in widening participation in the project by including children who may not have previously been interested or motivated to get involved. Taylor changed the way she carried out the research project by inviting children who had previously carried out projects to act as 'mentors' for the children in the current research group. This allowed her to involve six new young researchers who had all exhibited challenging behaviour in the classroom. Of these six children, one had a diagnosis of autism and one had a diagnosis of Attention Hyperactivity Disorder. By working in this way, Taylor was able to ensure that the project remained child led but that children who may have struggled to access the research activities were supported by their more experienced peers. The children chose to research the impact of the Forest School initiative in their Junior School. Two of the children did not want to attend the Young Researchers Conference because they were not comfortable with the idea of being in such a large group of people and presenting. However, these children were still very much involved in presenting the research as they were able to make contributions to the poster that was prepared to support the children's presentation. They were also able to be involved in sharing the findings with other adults in school, including governors.

Principles of participation

At the beginning of the Young Researchers Project, children and their teachers develop their research question(s). This can be problematic in terms of how the research question is arrived at. Many headteachers wish the children involved in the project to research an area that is linked to the School Development Plan. Although these may be of interest to the children as well as being part of the School Development Plan, there is a danger here of the teachers' agenda being forced onto the children, to arrive at research questions designed by adults, that run the risk of missing that which is relevant to the children (Kleine et al., 2016). Therefore, we have had to consider how participatory rights of children are managed effectively. Kleine et al. (2016) have guided us here, in terms of the notion of 'collective imagination'. Kleine et al. argue that the use of participatory methods encourages deeper levels of understanding of the community engaged in the research and a greater likelihood of impact longevity. This is endorsed by Kim (2016) who states that children are best placed to research the world of children, since they have a stronger experience and thus understanding of their own lives than adults. We have taken this premise and thought of its importance as we guide novice researchers; both teachers and children, towards developing mutually agreed and beneficial research questions. The nature of the Young Researchers Project resonates with key characteristics of participatory methods as voiced by Kleine (2016), for example:

Relevance
Flexibility
Empowerment
Creativity
Reflection.

Later in the book, we consider how each of our case studies links to these principles. However, as previously discussed, we would argue that our project is not about 'empowerment' as such, but about opening up a discursive space that allows the children's voices to be heard. We are also very aware of the importance of context in research. Although children are powerful conduits for the voices of their peer group, these groups are not homogenous. Our children are researching their own lived experiences and in this sense, a focus on local knowledge, local values and local issues can lead to more intuitive findings (Seballos & Tanner, 2009). Children's diversity of ideas, culture, identity, voice, class, ability and gender can impact on methods or approaches to participatory research (Kleine et al., 2016). As our case studies demonstrate, each teacher working with a group of children on the project takes a slightly different approach, depending on their knowledge of the children they are working with and the context in which they are working.

Success stories

Each year, we have been overwhelmed by the quality of research themes and questions explored by children as they present at the annual conference. Showcasing their findings reveals that children are indeed capable of owning and presenting meaningful research. Being challenged with creating poster presentations and having to respond to adult and child led questions on their findings has exemplified that children's research is indeed of relative quality to that of adults (Figures 3.1 and 3.2).

Most notable has been the ability of all children to grow in their understanding of the research process. This begins as early as the University Day, which is discussed in more detail in the next chapter. As the project progresses in each school, we see children increasingly demonstrating behaviours conducive with an understanding of the research process and the importance that this could have on change within their schools. They realise that they are making a difference, as reflected in the case study chapters later in this book. Murray (2016) also recognised this as part of her research, as anecdotal references to children's behaviours revealed children reflecting the behaviours of those adults who worked to inform policy and change. We also see

Figure 3.1: The Young Researchers Conference programme, front cover designed by a group of young researchers

Figure 3.2: A display of research materials on a presentation stand at the YRP conference

children involved in our project developing the skills and attributes highlighted by Cheminais (2012) in her work with children as action researchers, namely:

- Sense of pride and satisfaction in seeing the difference their projects have made
- Developing skills of communication, co-operation and self-confidence
- Developing critical thinking skills
- Gaining an understanding of how adults manage the decision-making process in school
- Improving skills in information technology.

The recognition of research behaviours in very young children has been highlighted by Clark and Moss (2011). Their work sought out the perspectives of the very young and the part that these played in informing effective practice. Once seen as unusual, their involvement of children as young as 22 months old reflects the ability of the youngest children to express preferences and communicate views. Previous work on developing children as researchers has tended to focus on children in the upper primary age range (for example, Bucknall, 2012; Cheminais, 2012). A key feature of the Young Researchers Project is that we have been successful in working with children as young as five years old. We have been mindful when considering research with the very young of the dangers of over facilitation by adults. It is important to go back to the principle that our role is to scaffold children's understanding of the research process and not to lead it. This approach is explored in more detail in Tara's case study in Chapter 6.

The success of the Young Researchers Project is also demonstrated by the fact that schools return annually to participate. The cumulative impact on schools that continue to participate in the project is illustrated in Chapter 5. French, Lowe and Nassem (2017) reported through their research that teachers recognised the involvement that children felt as they engaged in research and made decisions and changes to school policy and practice. The changes to policy and practice that have occurred as a result of the Young Researchers Project have been varied, from the development of a school kitchen garden, to changes in in the delivery of the school day, to changes to calculation polices for multiplication strategies. Such levels of involvement have impacted on teachers and children alike.

Several of the research projects have influenced policy decisions in individual schools. For example, in the project discussed in Chapter 5, children were invited to present their findings to the school's governing board, who then decided to make changes to the school grounds in line with the research findings. As the Young Researchers Project has progressed, there have been discussions surrounding the topic choice and a clear will on the part of the schools to engage in research on a broader level, beyond the individual school context. For example, the survival of the planet, local community spaces and homelessness have all been aired as potential areas for research. These research interests resonate with a social pedagogic view, in the sense that within these types of projects, children can consider their relationship with society. Through involvement in the research projects, children connect as citizens with a wider community and reflect and contribute to lifelong learning processes (Murphy & Joseph, 2019).

The Young Researchers Project is an ever-evolving programme. There are a number of emerging positive aspects of the project that we would like to explore in more detail in the future (see Chapter 10). In the next chapter, we will consider the role of university lecturers in the Young Researchers Project, in particular in their role as, 'research assistants'.

References

Biesta, G. J. J. (2007) Why 'what works' won't work. Evidence-based practice and the democratic deficit of educational research. *Educational Theory* Vol. 57, no. 1, pp. 1–22.

Bradbury-Jones, C., Taylor, J. (2015) Engaging with children as co-researchers: challenges, counter-challenges and solutions. *International Journal of Social Research Methodology* Vol. 18, no. 2, pp. 161–173.

Brooker, L. (2002) *Starting School: Young Children Learning Cultures*. Oxford University Press: Buckingham.

Bucknall, S. (2010) Children as researchers in English primary schools: developing a model for good practice. In: *British Educational Research Association Annual Conference*, 1–4 September 2010, University of Warwick, UK.

Bucknall, S. (2012) *Children as Researchers in Primary Schools: Choice, Voice and Participation*. Routledge: Abingdon.

Cheminais, R. (2012) *Children and Young People as Action Researchers: A Practical Guide to Supporting Pupil Voice in Schools*. Open University Press: Maidenhead.

Clark, A. & Moss, P. (2011) *Listening to Young Children: The Mosaic Approach*. 2nd edition. National Children's Bureau: London.

Clark, A. (2017) *Listening to Young Children: A Guide to Understanding and Using the Mosaic Approach*. Expanded 3rd edition. Jessica Kingsley Publishing: London.

Fraser, S., Lewis, V., Ding, S., Kellett, M. & Robinson, C. (2004) *Doing Research with Children and Young People*. Sage: London.

French, A., Lowe, R. & Nassem, E. (2017) Children participating in primary research schools: what's in it for teachers? *Education 3–13*. Vol. 47, no. 2, pp. 1–14.

Haw, K. F. (1996) Exploring the educational experiences of Muslim girls: tales told to tourists–should the white researcher stay at home? *British Educational Research Journal* Vol. 22, no. 3, pp. 319–329.

Kamler, B. & Thomson, P. (2008) The failure of dissertation advice books: towards alternative pedagogies for doctoral writing. *Educational Researcher* Vol. 37, no. 8, pp. 507–518.

Kellett, M. (2005) *Children as Active Researchers: A New Paradigm for the 21st Century*. Available at http://eprints.ncrm.ac.uk/87/1/MethodsReviewPaperNCRM-003.pdf [Accessed 30 August 2019].

Kim, C.-Y. (2016), Why research 'by' children? Rethinking the assumptions underlying the facilitation of children as researchers. *Child Soc* Vol. 30, pp. 230–240.

Kleine, D., Pearson, G. & Poveda, S. (2016) *Participatory Methods: Engaging Children's Voices and Experiences in Research*. Available at www.globalkidsonline.net/participatory-research [Accessed 30 August 2019].

Lyndon, H., Bertram, T., Brown, Z. & Pascal, C (2019) Pedagogically mediated listening practices: the development of pedagogy through the development of trust. *European Early Childhood Education Research Journal* Vol. 27, no. 3, pp. 360–370.

Murphy, D. & Joseph, S. (2019) Contributions from the person-centred experiential approach to the field of social pedagogy. *Cambridge Journal of Education* Vol. 49, no. 2, pp. 181–196.

Murray, J. (2014) Researching young children's worlds. In Waller, T. & Davis, G. (Eds.) *An Introduction to Early Childhood*. 3rd edition. Sage: London.

Murray, J. (2016) Young children are researchers: children aged four to eight years engage in important research behaviour when they base decisions on evidence. *European Early Childhood Education Research Journal* Vol. 4, no. 25, pp. 705–720.

Pascal, C. & Bertram, T. (2014) Transformative dialogues: the impact of participatory research on practice. In Clark, A., Flewitt, R., Hammersley, M. & Robb, M. (Eds.) *Understanding Research with Children and Young People*. Sage: London.

Seballos, F. & Tanner, T. (2009) The Importance of Participatory Child-Centred Research for Climate Adaptation. *IDS In Focus Policy Briefing* 13.6, IDS: Brighton.

Smith, N. (2014) Perspectives on parental involvement: a discussion of practitioner research. In Clark, A., Flewitt, R., Hammersley, M. & Robb, M. (Eds.) *Understanding Research with Children and Young People*. Sage: London.

United Nations (1989) *Convention on the Rights of the Child.* Available at https://downloads.unicef.org.uk/wp-content/uploads/2010/05/UNCRC_united_nations_convention_on_the_rights_of_the_child.pdf Accessed 28.08.2019 [Accessed 30 August 2019].

Wiliams, D. (2018) *Creating the Schools Our Children Need*. Learning Sciences International: West Palm Beach, US.

Chapter Four

Working together on the Young Researchers Project

Debbie Reel and Nicola Smith

This chapter will explore the value of developing partnerships between schools and universities and the mutual benefits that can emerge. In particular, it will examine our approach as university lecturers to working with children and teachers in the project. We will explore the place of the University Day and the Young Researchers Conference in the project and discuss our roles in these two important events, with consideration of our role as 'research assistants'. There will be a particular focus on the importance of a reciprocal relationship and parity in contributions from all involved in the research process. We will also consider more generally issues that relate to the developing partnerships beyond the Young Researchers project and the potential for their development.

Neutral spaces to develop new relationships

The Young Researchers Project partnership between University College Birmingham, University of Birmingham and and schools has been a welcome oasis in the current educational climate of accountability, economic survival and performance. Cornelissen, McLellan and Schofield (2017) make reference to the continual call for schools to work more collaboratively on research-informed projects to foster change. As discussed in the previous chapter, there is an expectation within the current education system for schools to engage more explicitly in research-led practice, in order to improve quality. Several schools recognise that a way in which this can be achieved is by working with universities. This is not a new concept and we would not consider ourselves pioneers in this area. However, the relationship that has built between the university and the lead school in particular and participating schools more generally has certainly created a positive impact amongst all involved.

Cornelissen et al. (2013) make reference to a research network that brings together schools and universities extending beyond the traditional focus on training teachers. As we develop this network, we have had to be cautious in determining what it is and what it may feel like to be a part of. As university lecturers, we have had to consider our roles and relationships to ensure equality and parity in the development of this relationship focussed on working with children as researchers. Bhabha (1994 cited in Jackson and Burch 2019) refers to the concept of third space. This highlights the importance of stepping outside of one's safe working environment. Arguably, by staying within the safety of what you know, the ability to exert power, consciously or not, may well be heightened. Being in a space that is new and neutral to all parties may instead create a sense of vulnerability and recognition that a shared, supportive and joint approach is needed. There is an increase in schools and universities acting as hybrids as a basis on which research can take place. We have been mindful to ensure that the hybrid created has not been one of hierarchy but rather of collaboration, communication and a developed understanding of different opportunities, providing time to carry out collaborative research that can impact on schools. Handscomb et al. (2014, p. 24) corroborate this as they refer to 'conditions for collaboration', emphasising the need for HEIs to consider changes to the ways in which they have traditionally worked.

Therefore, as academics working with teachers, we are concerned not with presenting ourselves as holding all of the knowledge but rather with supporting teachers in finding a neutral space and time to scaffold children's research projects. As discussed in the previous chapter, we see the Young Researchers Project as a space created for listening to the voices of participants, particularly those of children. Taking on the role of, 'research assistants', which will be discussed later in this chapter, has gone some way to address the potential of a power imbalance between university and school, dispelling the assumption that universities are the ones to lead research.

The Young Researchers Project has created the opportunity to develop a wide and encompassing research active community, in which we aim for equity in the research roles carried out. The creation of such a community, involving children, teachers and lecturers, aiming for equality in the process, has been described by Evans, Lomax and Morgan (2000, p. 410) as the 'magic paradox', where both a 'bottom up' and 'top down' approach are taken to working together. This magic paradox resonates with the concept of social pedagogic practice where rights, voices and contributions are equally valued. This concept of social pedagogy as part of the Young Researchers Project is discussed further in Chapter 10. We have come to realise, through research and action, that there is no 'one way' to carry out research with children and there is no fixed partnership model. What has remained as a constant, however, is our understanding of a neutral and flexible working model that is shaped by the experiences of all involved in the process with whom we work each year.

School and university partnership: developing our research active community

The relationship between Colmore Partnership Teaching School Alliance, University College Birmingham, The University of Birmingham and young researchers across Birmingham schools has grown out of the dedication of Viv Randal. Her role as headteacher gave a platform to promote the importance of children representing themselves and having the agency to do so. As explored in Chapter 2, Viv was interested in challenging the assumption that young children cannot carry out real research in comparison with an adult and that the research findings produced by them cannot be deemed as reliable as those produced by adult researchers. Indeed, Kim, Sheehy and Kerawall (2017, p. 234) corroborate this research dilemma stating:

> Where adults have been impressed by the quality of children's research, it is unknown whether this was because it was better than what they might have expected from 'a child' or whether 'adult' research of a similar quality would have impressed them just the same.

The value of school and university partnerships has already been voiced and remains well documented (Passy, Georgeson, & Gompertz 2018; Walsh & Backe 2013). It was UCB's already secure partnership with the CPTSA that enhanced our collaboration promoting the Young Researchers Project. Walsh and Backe (2013) refer to the changing landscape on which school/university partnerships are based, as there is now a shift towards the needs of schools acting as the deter-miner for the partnership rather than the needs of the university. This is the approach that we have taken in the Young Researchers Project; what do the schools need that we, as academics working in a university context, are able to provide? We framed our responses to this question in relation to what we could add in terms of the quality of the research. Our starting point was the children, since they are at the centre of the Young Researchers Project. We knew that we needed to listen to the voices of children in the Young Researchers Project and share with them the value of research. For example, Chappell et al. (2008) refer to the approach taken by pre-schools in Reggio Emilia through learning, researching and enquiring together. Our role in the Young Researchers Project is one of learn-ing, researching and enquiring alongside the children and teachers.

As stated by Walkington (2007), reciprocity must be part of the research process. If we want to be learning, researching and enquiring together, then we need to meet together at the beginning of the research project and thus the 'University Day' was introduced. The University Day has been instrumental in developing children and staff's understanding of how they can meaningfully engage in the research process, raising aspirations and building on children's experiences and understanding, acknowledging that they are all researchers as they ask questions and seek answers.

Exploring ethics, meaningful research questions, and qualitative and quantita-tive research, the University Day has been pitched at a level to which children can aspire. It also dispels any myths that research only takes place in universities by 'academics'. Acknowledging this, Harcourt and Einarsdottir (2011, p. 304) state that '…when they are treated as equals, all young children can take owner-ship and actively participate in every stage of the research process'. Our aim is that young researchers leave the University Day enthused and confident that they are able to carry out research. Cheeseman and Walker (2019) make reference to the child as a researcher in the form of an explorer making sense of the world and those in it. It is this premise that sets the basis for the University Day where children are encouraged to recognise their ability to lead research, ask questions and generate a range of answers, which in essence is something that children do daily.

Key Features of the University Day

- Young researchers are welcomed into a university environment where they are given the opportunity to see and feel what a university is like.
- The key aim is to introduce children to research processes including research questions, the importance of ethics, differences between quantitative and qualitative research and research strategies. All of this is delivered so that children can access and gain a better understanding of the process, with child centred audience participation included.
- A further aim for this day is to dispel myths that research only takes place in a university by academics.
- The atmosphere is informal, we share breakfast and the children familiarise themselves with the new environment in a relaxed manner before the 'official' part of the day begins.
- In a large lecture theatre we present a short child centred session on research covering aspects such as:

What does it mean to be a researcher? What does a researcher do? How can a researcher find things out? How can a researcher make sure that they act fairly and ask the right questions to the right participants?

- There is also input from a librarian as to their role and how children can carry out effective literature searches.
- The role of university academics as 'research assistants' for the literature review is introduced and explained.
- The pitch is designed to engage all children who leave the lecture theatre as detectives ready to find answers to the questions they have set.

The Young Researchers Conference and inclusion

When we first became involved with the Young Researchers Project, most of the children involved were amongst the most articulate and confident in their year group, as referred to in Chapter 2. Teachers tended to select these children for involvement in the project with a view to presenting findings at the conference at the end of the year. The research projects are subject to the time pressures that most teachers are operating under and, understandably, they want to be sure that their projects will be successful in the limited time available. However, in terms of the aim of the Young Researchers Project to develop a 'discursive space' where children's voices can be heard, the project needed to be more inclusive, particularly in relation to including children who are not confident speakers. One of the things we have done to address this is to change the format of the conference, whilst still keeping it as close to a 'proper' research conference as possible. Instead of standing up in front of everyone and presenting their research findings, now the children create a research poster for the conference and answer questions from conference delegates in a more informal manner. This has given teachers confidence to include children who may be less used to speaking in a formal setting. We have also seen teachers such as Taylor, included in Chapter 3, working with children with challenging behaviour on research projects, supported by more experienced child researchers as their mentors.

Like Taylor, all adults involved in the project need to be open to seeing ideas from new perspectives, which can be challenging but has the potential to impact profoundly on professional development. The success of the Young Researchers Project in providing a discursive space may largely depend on how inclusive adults are and their depth of reflexivity about their influence upon the children. This is one of the reasons why regular meeting are important, so that adult participants can reflect on the progress of the projects and on their own role in the research. Over the course of the school year, all of the adults involved in the project meet up on a regular basis, to share progress and to discuss any stumbling blocks in the research. This also provides an opportunity for schools to make links with one another in order to carry out research beyond their own individual school context, as discussed later in the case study chapters.

In order to further support an inclusive research practice offered by teachers and lecturers, as academics we have developed our role in the Young Researchers Project as research assistants. The purpose of this has been two fold. First, this 'job title' challenges the potential for us to be viewed as the university academics who hold all of the knowledge. The term research assistant emphasises the creation of a shared research space that is beneficial to all. Second, this choice of title relates to an issue that arose early on in the Young Researchers Project, concerned with children's ability to access previous research in their chosen area. This is not to suggest that children cannot understand the area for research, simply that the educational research literature is not aimed at children, causing a stumbling block in understanding content and context when carrying out any review of literature – a fundamental part of research. In our initial discussions with Viv around our role in the project, it was decided that we would act as research assistants for the children and create research digests based on their chosen areas. Once again, we had to reflect here on our role in this part of the project. We had to be mindful that, as adults, we did not impose our own thoughts and views on the research literature but present it in as truthful a manner as possible. Our backgrounds as former primary teachers and presently as university lecturers in childhood education were important in bringing child appropriate understanding and relevance to the research questions whilst trying to remain unbiased in our approach. Dickson and Green (2001) recognise this challenge and state that all research is subject to 'ideology and biases' (p. 245). We have worked on the Dickson and Green (2001) premise that our role as research assistants is instructive and designed to enable children to carry out research that is relative in quality to that of adults. As 'research assistants' for the children's projects, we are able to ensure that children can access and understand research that has previously been carried out in the field. From an ethical point of view, there are several issues to consider in relation to this role. As 'gatekeepers' to published research, we have to ensure that we conduct a thorough literature search and do not present research to children that has been filtered through the lens of our own interests and biases. We also have to be careful that in presenting research in ways that children can understand, we are not 'dumbing down', or misrepresenting the evidence in any way. This has certainly allowed us as lecturers to consider our own practice and to develop professionally as we have had to consider how literature is presented, how we can influence this and how to deal with literature that could cause concern for some. This is discussed with particular relevance to the case study from Kings Heath Primary in Chapter 7.

Professional development through collaborative partnerships

Teachers involved in the project have had different experiences of carrying out research. Some have completed master's level work in education or other fields, but others may not have been involved in reading or writing about research since they completed an undergraduate dissertation. For almost all of the children involved in the Young Researchers Project, this was their first involvement in carrying out a research study and, for us, these children are already on the journey of 'being and becoming' researchers.

The benefits of the of the Young Researchers Project for children are discussed throughout this book, but here we focus on the positive impact on teachers. Walkington (2007, p. 286) refers to the connection between schools and universities and how this can create an immediate sense of 'professional growth'. Through our experiences to date, supporting teachers within the project has broadened their engagement with the development of their schools and enabled them to share findings with headteachers, parents and governors. For example, in Chapter 5 we consider how the professional experiences of staff at Lyndon Green Infant School have been extended as different teachers take on responsibility for the development of a research-active school.

Teachers have managed different groups of children through the process of research and developed in their understanding of stepping back and listening to the child. This has ensured that the findings from the research are real. They have met regularly with other teachers and heads, liaised and visited other schools analysing alternative practices and sharing ideas. Cheng and So (2012) refer to the limitations of relying on one's own experiences, as this narrow approach can limit development. They examine studies that focus on partnerships between schools and universities and how these meaningfully impact on teachers' pedagogic practice. The case studies documented in later chapters demonstrate the impact that involvement in the school–university partnership has had on teachers and how they have developed professionally.

This development has not been ad hoc and, for those teachers who have been part of the Young Researchers Project, the professional development and its impact on confidence and knowledge is tangible, bringing us back to the concept of reciprocity. The importance of mutuality and the benefits of a collaborative approach are most clearly advocated during regular meetings with teachers and the university lecturers. Aubusson, Ewing and Hoban (2009, cited in Cheng and So, 2012) refer to an initial lack of knowledge based around structuring research discussion groups: their form and function. However, the professional dialogue in which we engage acts as a backbone to the Young Researchers Project overall. This is where we come together as a team, share ideas, concerns and ways forward, structure next steps and plan ahead. This opportunity for professional dialogue allows the teachers a voice and a chance to think and to be questioned critically, yet supportively about their children's research and their role in the process. This in itself contributes to teachers developing professionally.

But what of the more formal benefits to teachers' professional development? Over the years of the Young Researchers Project, the prospect of certification for participation and engagement has often been discussed, however, we are acutely aware that the professional engagement and the development of staff needs to be more professionally recognised. As universities, we offer masters programmes in learning and teaching, all of which attract existing teachers who wish to further develop in academic attainment. The possibility of creating a partnership with schools that support not only young researchers but also teachers to engage in masters study is a viable prospect. The relationship formed between a university and a school as part of young researchers can be seen as a stepping stone to further study as described by Cornelissen et al. (2013). As you will read in Chapter 6, the experiences of Tara as the research lead teacher demonstrate how she has used her experience as an MA researcher to develop that of the young researchers in her class.

As part of the aforementioned University Day, children are guided through the research process. This is delivered in a child-accessible format, yet describes the exact process with which adult researchers engage. The relationships formed and the structure of the Young Researchers process resonates with the key point made by Cornelissen et al. (2013, p. 37) that 'relational and structural dimensions' need to be considered when developing partnerships and supporting meaningful professional development. The opportunity to embed findings from engagement with the Young Researchers Project into a teacher's master's research is a possibility and would support the relational dimension previously discussed.

Currently, those teachers engaging in master's study may make individual decisions as to the content of their research with university support throughout the process. It is envisaged that a teacher could use their experiences of the Young Researchers Project to develop further and experience a shift to a more relational opportunity where their lived experiences matter and are built into the programme. This would encourage professional development based around the ongoing research needs and interests of the school with a reciprocal level of support between school and university. This closely ties with the work of Lave and Wenger (Walton et al. 2019) who refer to the importance of learning communities developing learning as a social practice. In support, reference to the work of Duncombe and Armour (2004) relates to collaborative professional learning in which they refer to the 'tacit knowledge' of teachers (p. 144). They firmly believe that there is untapped knowledge held by teachers that has not been made relevant or valued and that there is the danger of that which we call collaboration really being a masquerade for domination of views and ideas on behalf of the more knowledgeable other. Building on a reciprocal and constructive approach to developing teachers as researchers has the potential to enhance any university master's programme. This would allow for the creation of a professional platform in which teachers and universities can mutually contribute, based on their lived experiences of the Young Researchers Project that are real and relevant to their everyday practice.

Within this chapter we have considered the opportunities that meaningful partnerships between schools and universities can create and the role that a Young Researchers Project in any school may play in this development. The main theme has been that of equity and parity amongst all involved and an awareness of the tacit knowledge that, if tapped into, can create new opportunities for collaborative professional development.

References

Chappell, K., Craft, A., Burnard, P. & Cremin, T. (2008) Question-posing and question-responding: the heart of 'Possibility Thinking' in the early years. *Early Years* Vol. 28, no. 3, pp. 267–286.

Cheng, M. & So, W. (2012) Analysing teacher professional development through professional dialogue: an investigation into a university-school partnership project on enquiry learning. *Journal of Education for Teaching* Vol. 38, no. 3, pp. 323–341.

Cheeseman, S. & Walker, R. (2019) *Pedagogies for Leading Practice*. Routledge: Abingdon.

Cornelissen, F., Daly, A., Liou, Y., van Swet, J., Beijaard, D. & Bergen, T. (2013) More than a master: developing, sharing, and using knowledge in school-university research networks. *Cambridge Journal of Education* Vol. 44, no. 1, pp. 35–57.

Cornelissen, F., McLellan, R. & Schofield, J. (2017) Fostering research engagement in partnership schools: networking and value creation. *Oxford Review of Education* Vol. 43, no. 6, pp. 695–717.

Dickson, G. & Green, K. (2001) The external researcher in participatory action research. *Educational Action Research* Vol. 9, no. 2, pp. 243–260.

Duncombe, R. & Armour, K. (2004) Collaborative professional learning: from theory to practice. *Journal of In-Service Education* Vol. 30, no. 1, pp. 141–166.

Evans, M., Lomax, P. & Morgan, H. (2000) Closing the circle: action research partnerships towards better learning and teaching in schools. *Cambridge Journal of Education* Vol. 30, no. 3, pp. 405–419.

Handscomb, G., Gu, Q. & Varley, M. (2014) School-university partnerships: fulfilling the potential. Available at https://www.publicengagement.ac.uk/sites/default/files/publication/literature_review_final.pdf (Accessed 19 December 2019).

Harcourt, D. & Einarsdottir, J. (2011) Introducing children's perspectives and participation in research. *European Early Childhood Education Research Journal* Vol. 19, no. 3, pp. 301–307.

Jackson, A. & Burch, J. (2019) New directions for teacher education: investigating school/university partnership in an increasingly school based context. *Professional Development in Education* Vol. 45, no. 1, pp. 138–150.

Kim, C., Sheehy, K. & Kerawall, L. (2017) *Developing Children as Researchers: A Practical Guide to Help Children Conduct Social Research.* Routledge: Oxon.

Passy, R., Georgeson, J. & Gompertz, B. (2018) Building learning partnerships between schools and universities: an example from south-west England. *Journal of Education for Teaching* Vol. 44, no. 5, pp. 539–555.

Walkington, J. (2007) Improving partnerships between schools and universities: professional learning with benefits beyond pre service education. *Teacher Development* Vol. 11, no. 3, pp. 227–294.

Walsh, M.E. & Backe, S. (2013) School–University partnerships: reflections and opportunities. *Peabody Journal of Education* Vol. 88, no. 5, pp. 594–607.

Walton, E., Carrington, S., Saggers, B., Edwards, C. & Kimani, W. (2019) What matters in learning communities for inclusive education: a cross-case analysis. *Professional Development in Education* pp. 1–15.

Chapter Five

Young researchers in action

Lyndon Green Infant School

Kerry Orme

Introduction

Lyndon Green Infant School has been involved with the Young Researchers Project for over five years. The projects carried out at the school have all had a lasting impact on practice and on the school environment.

To begin with, I recruited children from the 'Gifted and Talented' group of pupils in school. The project was seen to be a good way to challenge their thinking of high-attaining pupils and to allow them to have the opportunity to develop their own ideas and skills in terms of working in and leading groups. More recently though, all children have been invited to submit an application to become a young researcher. Applicants are chosen to be part of the team if they have a particular interest in a project's focus or if they demonstrate that they would be able to utilise research skills and talk about the project at the Young Researchers Conference. Our young researchers have made changes to the way I run the project over the last few years. For example, originally we would have our young researchers' meetings at lunchtimes but children did not like missing out on opportunities to spend time with their friends. A group decision was made to hold the meeting during teaching sessions in the school day instead. As we are an infant school, our young researchers are typically aged five, six and seven.

Research questions

Research questions are usually linked to school priorities and the improvement plan in any given year. Although this puts some limitations on what children can research, in terms of practicalities it means that it is easier to allocate sufficient time to the project during the year. At Lyndon Green, doing the research project properly and devoting enough time to carry out meaningful research are seen as priorities. Once the research focus has been decided, children lead the project as much as possible. This means that they will come up with particular research questions in relation to a school priority. However, in our most recent project, the young researchers decided that they wanted to focus on how they feel at school, as this was an area that they were interested in. As a consequence, this project explored wellbeing and what we could do as a school to promote and/or improve this aspect of children's lives. A summary of our research, including the research questions, can be seen in Figure 5.1, the poster we presented at the Young Researchers Conference.

Methodology

Over the years, children have developed expertise in a number of different research methods. We have used questionnaires and interviews to collect data from children

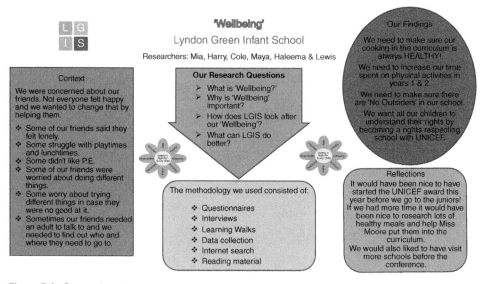

Figure 5.1: Research poster

and adults in school. Other methods such as 'learning walks', where we visit class-rooms around school and observe what is happening in them, have also proved useful. We have found that planning time for library and computer access is very important in relation to methodological considerations. For example, when researching the effectiveness of our 'Scoot to School' initiative, children were able to use data from the school office to draw graphs using a computer package when organising and analysing their data. I have also found that visiting other schools to research how they approach particular areas of focus can be very helpful, as well as keeping children motivated and engaged in their research projects.

Findings

As the projects have all been focused on children's experiences at school, there have always been practical implications of our research findings. This has meant that every project has led to changes in practice and often in the physical environment, too. All of the projects carried out at Lyndon Green can still be seen to have an impact in school. For example, we still have a kitchen garden which is used to grow ingredients for our lunchtime salad bar as a result of our project on healthy eating in school. Children in Year 1 are all given scooter training as a result of our research into the 'Scoot to School' initiative. We have found that the biggest impact is made by those projects that are centred on things that our children take part in day to day e.g. travelling to school; playing outside; eating healthily. The project that has had some of the biggest impact has been that of our research into Forest School. We now have three different Forest School spaces on the school site, one for each year group, with two Forest School leaders who take children out to Forest School dur-ing teachers' PPA time. The leaders are a trained teacher and Higher Level Teaching Assistant, demonstrating the commitment to this area of learning in our school since the original young researchers project was carried out. The Forest School research has influenced practice throughout the school, with staff INSET sessions exploring outdoor learning and parents being involved in Forest School sessions on a regular basis.

Another project that has had a strong influence on our practice looked at the implementation of Guy Claxton's (2002) 'Building Learning Power' ideas in our teaching sessions, including the 'Four Rs'; Resilience, Resourcefulness, Reflectiveness and Reciprocity. This project found that these strategies were working well at Lyndon Green and so we have continued to use them and to develop the approach further. For example, we have introduced a half termly reward assembly to recognise those children who are using the 'Learning Powers' effectively.

The findings of our most recent research project can be seen on the conference poster in Figure 5.1.

Reflections

I have found the Young Researchers Project to be an effective way of developing children's knowledge and skills as well as those of adults. Having overseen the projects for a number of years, I have now handed over this role to another member of staff. In this way, the Young Researchers Project is a staff development opportunity as well as being a powerful vehicle for listening to children in our school. Parents at Lyndon Green are also enthusiastic supporters of the Young Researchers Project. As the children have to make an application to be a young researcher, taking part in the project is recognised as an achievement in itself. Parents also value the link with universities and appreciate the aspirational element of the project that this brings. Our young researchers have presented their findings to the headteacher, governors and their peers, as well as talking about the project to Ofsted inspectors. Thus the impact of the projects goes beyond the influence of any individual project and can be seen in children's increased confidence in public speaking, stronger relationships between stakeholders in school and an increase in the school's influence in the local community.

Commentary

Children's voice at Lyndon Green

Beyond the idea of the Young Researchers Project opening up a space for the voices of children at Lyndon Green to be heard, the children have been involved in shaping and changing that space as the project has developed over the years. Children have changed the way that the project is organised by moving from lunchtime meetings to planning their research as part of the school day. This may appear to be a small change but for young children at Key Stage One, there are few opportunities to have any control over how their school days are organised. Bucknall (2012, p. 11) stresses the particular importance of, 'choice as an expression of voice' for young researchers and here children are exercising their choice of when the group should meet. By allowing children to influence the organisation of the Young Researchers Project in this way, Kerry is demonstrating that adults are serious about listening to children in the school and supporting them as they co-construct their research projects.

The children at Lyndon Green are some of the youngest children involved in the Young Researchers Project and so it is particularly important that they can see the concrete results of their voices being heard. The Forest School areas, scooter parking and kitchen garden serve as a constant reminder that children in the school have been listened to and action taken as a result of their research. Kerry writes about the importance of carrying out the research 'properly'. There is obvious importance here in relation to the credibility of the research but this is also important from the children's point of view. This commitment to meaningful research is further evidence that children are being taken seriously, as members of the school community and as young researchers, avoiding tokenism in listening to their voices (Alderson, 2017). This commitment is underlined by the involvement of presentations to all stakeholders in school, as well as by encouraging children to talk about their projects to visiting Ofsted inspectors.

Kerry writes about the parents' perceptions of the Young Researchers Project and this is another important aspect of the work at Lyndon Green. Much has been written about the importance of parental engagement in primary education and by considering parent points of view, Lyndon Green are demonstrating the worth of the Young Researchers Project beyond the school gates. These young researchers are taking an active role in shaping their own lives and those of others in their community and thus demonstrating agency in relation to their social worlds (James and Prout, 2015).

Children's participation at Lyndon Green

The Young Researchers Project at Lyndon Green can be seen to embrace all of Kleine et al.'s (2016) principles of participatory research, but in particular there is an emphasis on **relevance** and **participation**. As Kerry reflects, the most successful projects are those that have resulted in changes to school life and environment that remain visible to the children. Clark (2010) reminds us that listening to children can mean opening up areas of research that adults might miss. Working with a particular agenda, in many cases the school development plan, can mean that as adults we only hear information that relates to this agenda. This was illustrated at Lyndon Green, when the children decided to research wellbeing, which had not previously been included as part of the school development plan or suggested as a potential research project. It is significant that Kerry allowed the children to research wellbeing, which they deemed more relevant to their own lives than any area on the school development plan. In doing so, the children were able to influence and co-construct the research according to their own agenda (Kleine et al., 2016).

The continuation of projects such as the kitchen garden, forest school and scooter projects allows all children in the school to feel ownership of the results of the Young Researchers Project, not just those who carried out the original research. Kerry's approach to the Young Researchers Project and the length of time for which the school has been involved combine to mean that the work of young researchers is embedded in the ethos of the school. The projects at Lyndon Green underline the importance of the support and active involvement of senior leaders in school and the embedding of the projects into whole school approaches, as discussed by Viv in Chapter 2.

References

Alderson, P. (2017) Children as researchers: The effects of participation rights on research methodology, in Christensen, P. and James, A. (Eds), *Research with Children: Practices and Perspectives*. Routledge: Abingdon.

Bucknall, S. (2012) *Children as Researchers in Primary Schools: Choice, Voice and Participation*. Routledge: Abingdon.

Clark, A. (2010) *Transforming Children's Spaces: Children's and Adults' Participation in Designing Learning Environments*. Routledge: Abingdon.

Claxton, G. (2002) *Building Learning Power*. TLO Ltd: Bristol.

James, A. and Prout, A. (2015) *Constructing and Reconstructing Childhood: Contemporary Issues in the Sociological Study of Childhood*. Routledge: Abingdon.

Kleine, D., Pearson, G., and Poveda, S. (2016) *Participatory Methods: Engaging Children's Voices and Experiences in Research*. Available at www.globalkidsonline.net/participatory-research [Accessed 30 August 2019].

Chapter Six

Young researchers in action

The Oaks Primary School

Tara Harris

Introduction

I am a teacher currently working at The Oaks Primary School in Druids Heath. Druids Heath is located on the outskirts of South Birmingham and is a 1960s purpose-built council estate. In 2019 The Oaks had the third highest number of pupils (85%) on roll eligible for pupil premium in England.

Despite these adversities, or because of them, the children at our school have a strong sense of autonomy, justice and a huge capacity for resilience. The governors, senior leaders and staff have created a school that allows children to interact in a diverse school community with inclusivity, respect and empathy.

When I became involved in the Young Researchers Project, I had already been accepted to participate in the Teacher Leader course run by Ambitions Institute. Part of the course was to develop a research question focused on raising pupil attainment. The Ambitions Institute signposted me to use the Educational Endowment Foundation Toolkit (EEF, 2018). The Educational Endowment Foundation is an independent charity that provides evidence-based research and resources to teachers and senior leaders. I became interested in their resource about meta-cognition and self-regulation approaches. I discovered that studies in this area indicated that meta-cognitive learning was particularly beneficial for pupils from low-income families. The evaluation of their studies found gains, on average, of an additional eight months progress. Meta-cognitive knowledge is defined as what we know about ourselves as a thinker and learner (EEF, 2018). The characteristics of a meta-cognitive classroom that I wanted to develop were developing a language for thinking and sustained dialogue between the children and adults about thinking and learning.

In the academic year 2016 to 2017, the children in Year 1 took part in the Young Researchers Project. I chose a team of five children who were five and six years of age. Each child had different strengths and I chose them not for their academic abilities but on each child's potential to demonstrate curiosity and develop critical thinking. As I was also doing my own research project I needed to demonstrate that using a research project could impact on raising attainment. All the children chosen were either on track or below age related expectations. I felt that the Young Researchers Project would have a significant impact on children and would increase attainment over a sustained period. At the start of the academic year, I got to know my new class and began considering which children would make a good research team. The first to be chosen was Miriam. Miriam had boundless energy and her infectious enthusiasm would mean the team would never rest on their laurels. Tyrone made original and slightly off-the-wall observations in class discussion. He had the humour and creativity needed for the team. I noted the potential for Rudania to develop her social skills by becoming part of the team. She found making friends difficult and was a keen contributor to our class discussions. Bobby was quietly confident and considered others' viewpoints and Zubair was a quiet, hardworking child and good friends with Tyrone. I made sure that the other children in the class understood that although they had not been selected for the research team who would attend the University Day and conference, they were part of the larger class team of researchers. Some research was planned and delivered as whole class lessons to involve all of the children in our Young Researchers Project.

Previous research

The initial idea of a research question was based on my own research using the Educational Endowment Foundation Toolkit (EEF, 2018), which identified that meta-cognition and self- regulation strategies could accelerate progress particularly for low achieving pupils. The research question 'How do Children Learn?' was formulated from this research. The aim was that the team could use research methods to find out which types of learning behaviour was taking place around the school.

I started by asking my Year 1 class the question 'How do you learn?' The answers were pretty disastrous, in the sense that children did not focus on learning. The majority of children said things that were behaviour based. For example, 'You learn by sitting up straight and putting your finger on your lips.' This was a worry for me. How could I ask my newly formed team to research 'How Children Learn?' if they did not understand what learning was? I realised that these younger researchers needed an understanding of the question they were about to research. So I used my plenaries in lesson time differently. Each and every plenary, I asked the children to reflect on the research question, 'How did you learn?' They were introduced to selected meta-cognitive words to use when explaining and I modelled how to use them. For example: 'Today, you have learned by taking turns and showing each other your work.' Soon, the children were able to explain how they learned. They had increased the language of learning to include the following vocabulary;

- finding out
- showing others
- taking turns
- having a go
- thinking
- using imagination
- checking
- sharing
- testing
- choosing
- deciding
- looking for patterns
- solving problems
- exploring
- playing
- taking care
- remembering other learning
- finding out.

There are other learning words but these were the ones I felt were appropriate to this year group. A few months later the children were able to use these terms when reflecting on their learning.

Research questions

At the start of the project I quickly discovered, during circle time sessions, that the whole class struggled to distinguish between a question and an answer. I needed to explicitly teach this skill for the team to be able to formulate personal research questions. At The Oaks we use the Philosophy for Children approach (SAPERE, 1992). At the core of this approach is enabling children to think of their own questions and explore them. Using this approach once a week ensured that children were being asked to think of questions based on stimuli like a book or a picture. In addition, the English Primary Curriculum for Year One (DfE, 2013) has objectives that are based on questioning. This meant that there were several lessons where the Year 1 team taught questioning as distinct lessons. Using Reciprocal Reading (Fischer Family Trust, 2018) also encouraged the children to think of their own questions about what they had read, in the designated role of Questioner.

When the children had mastered the concept of questioning, each member came up with their own question. Although I had led the initial question for the research project, I felt that it was important for the children to lead their own line of enquiry now. This strategy involved them becoming more active participants. They took on the responsibility of planning, decision making, evaluating and implementing the project.

The children's questions can be seen in Table 6.1

Methodology and findings

As a whole class we made a meta-word grid, which was displayed in the classroom and used as a reference in class introductions and plenaries. Words on the grid included connections, looking and finding patterns. For the individual questions, children decided on their own research methods, all using this meta-word resource in different ways.

Table 6.1 Research questions

Whole team question	How do children learn in Year 1?
Miriam	How do children learn in Year 2?
Zubair	How do children learn when they are playing?
Bobby	How do you learn in PE?
Rukhsana	Why are you learning?
Tyrone	Do you always have to sit on chairs to learn in Years 5 and 6?

Miriam: How do children learn in Year 2?

Miriam's chosen method of collecting evidence was to use the meta-word grid as voting tool. She gave all the children in Year 2 the opportunity to tick their top three ways of learning. With my support, we collated these. Miriam noticed the most popular, 'I saw that they like having a go, checking work and trying out new things the best.'

Zubair: How do children learn when they are playing?

Zubair wanted his friend Tyrone to help him with his research question. The boys asked adults the question first and they recorded adult responses on a questionnaire sheet. They then spent time watching the children during their lesson, although some of this time was spent joining in with the irresistible Reception activities. They then read the meta-word grid and selected the words that they had observed in the children's play. In conclusion Zubair said, 'The children were exploring and using their imagination, so I think that is how they are learning.'

Rukhsana: Why are you learning?

With adult support, Rukhsana asked this question to different children throughout the school. Their answers were recorded and played back with common themes arising. Radaina's summary of her finding was, 'The children said, "If you don't learn you won't know how to do things. You can't have a house. You won't be able to do SATs. You won't be clever and know things."'

Bobby: How do children learn in PE?

Bobby simply observed a PE lesson and each time she saw an example of meta-learning she ticked it on the meta-word grid. In this way Bobby was able to discover that lots of the learning was done by listening to the instructor. She also commented, 'I saw them having a go, taking turns and being part of a team.' I sat next to Bobby just to check that she was not just ticking words off randomly and she told me what she had seen.

There were challenges in supporting the young children, one of which was time. I was lucky enough to be able to take the group or individuals out during several afternoon sessions. During this focused time I was surprised at how seriously the children were in collecting information and how able they were at arriving at their findings with minimum support.

Reflections

A year on from the project, the children in Year 1 and the Young Researcher Team continue to amaze their teachers. They are exuberant confident learners who are able to ask pertinent questions and delve deeper to find the answers. Children who were below attainment in reading, writing and maths are now on target to meet expected outcomes. Four children have gone on to attain greater depth in reading and maths. Rukhsana has developed her social skills and Zubair is not so quiet anymore. Bobby and Tyrone were accepted for the Birmingham Royal Ballet and continue to attend every Monday. Miriam continues to be bright and eager to learn and now motivates others to do their best. The children remember the project and visit me often in my classroom. I think this is because we spent so much time together doing something that was personal and meaningful.

I am now teaching in Year 2 and am using child-centred, enquiry-based approaches to develop our young researchers for the future. I intend to ask open questions as starting points for class topics. The children will come up with their own research questions and spend curriculum time researching. Lessons will be fluid and child-led which will strengthen children's capacity to think creativity, critically and collaboratively.

Commentary

Children's voice at the Oaks

The voices of the children at the Oaks are clearly captured in this case study, as the research questions and summaries of findings are included as spoken by the children. Leat and Reid (2012, pp. 190) highlight a range of non-cognitive benefits that emerge from young children engaging in the research process. These include:

A sense of self agency
An inquiring mind
New social competencies and relationships
Reflection on learning
The opportunity to be active and creative.

We can see all these benefits illustrated when we listen to the voices of the young researchers at The Oaks. All the children are reflecting on learning, as this is the focus of their project and their voices are powerful in demonstrating how they link what they observed with what they know about meta-cognition e.g. Zubair knows how to recognise when children are using imagination and he can reflect on this in relation to learning. The children's inquiring minds and sense of self-agency are evident in their competence in framing their own research question. Zubair and Tyrone build on their relationship as they carry out research together. Tara's reflections note the development of social competencies in two of the children in particular.

Cheminais (2012, p. 3) reminds us that 'Children have the expert knowledge of what it is like to be a child, not adults.' The voices of the children from the Oaks express this expertise; for example, Miriam is able to identify the most popular ways of learning in Year 2. She is able to communicate this expertise using the language of meta-cognition that Tara has developed with her class. In this way she has been supported to develop her expertise on meta-cognition and link this to her expertise about children's experiences in school.

Children's participation at the Oaks

This case study particularly reflects the principles of **creativity, flexibility** and **reflection** (Kleine et al., 2016). By allowing children to select their own research methods (e.g. Miriam asking children to choose their top three learning methods; Rukhsana asking her question and recording the answers), Tara made sure that the children remained motivated and were able to communicate freely with their research participants. In allowing creative responses to the research design, Tara enables the young researchers to demonstrate their capabilities as researchers. Rukhsana demonstrates her competence as a young researcher by identifying common themes in participants' answers and summarising them accurately. Miriam shows that she is co-shaping and influencing the research by using the meta-word grid as a voting tool and thus identifying children's most preferred ways of learning, adding another layer of analysis to the study. The research processes are open and responsive, as typified in Tara's response to the children's initial lack of understanding of the research question. This flexible approach means that the young researchers are supported to develop their research skills, as Tara thinks carefully about what they need to underpin their understanding.

Tara's writing about how she chose the team for the Young Researchers Project demonstrates the principle of reflection on the part of the adult involved in the research. She thinks carefully about which children will benefit from the project and this child-led approach is apparent throughout the case study. This demonstrates how much adults thinking has developed in comparison with the 'show and tell' approach to children's research that Viv discussed in Chapter 2. The children at The Oaks demonstrate that they are able to reflect on what they have seen in the classroom and how this might link to ideas on meta-cognition. By using the meta-words grid, the children are able to understand the complexities of meta-cognition in an accessible way and reflect on these in relation to learning in their school.

It can be argued that for this project, the principle of **relevance** is linked to the teacher's priorities more than to those of the children. After all, Tara chose to research this area because of her own interest in the findings of the EEF meta-analysis (EEF, 2018). However, looking more closely at this principle and the way in which it is interwoven with the other principles, Tara's flexible and creative approach meant that the project was carried out in such a way that the children could relate to the topic and build their own meanings around it, for example by formulating their own questions and making their own choices of research methods. Thus the children influenced and shaped the research as it progressed from the suggested starting point, allowing them as young researchers to participate and lead the project in a meaningful way. The children at The Oaks are some of our youngest researchers, but in this case study have demonstrated the ways in which they are 'becoming and belonging' (Kamler and Thomson, 2008) as part of our research community, developing their understanding of how to form research questions and how to analyse data. If we go back to our discussion of children's competence as researchers in Chapter 3, Tara's role in at The Oaks is to follow Bucknall's (2010) approach of scaffolding her young research team. Some of this scaffolding is in the form of direct teaching (e.g. teaching about questions in the English curriculum); some is in the form of resources (e.g. the meta-words grid) and some is in the form of support (sitting alongside Bobby as she carries out her data collection).

References

Bucknall, S. (2010) Children as researchers in English primary schools: Developing a model for good practice. In: *British Educational Research Association Annual Conference*, 1–4 September 2010, University of Warwick, UK.

Cheminais, R. (2012) *Children and Young People as Action Researchers: A Practical Guide to Supporting Pupil Voice in Schools*. Open University Press: Maidenhead.

Education Endowment Foundation (2018) *Sutton Trust-Education Endowment Foundation Teaching and Learning Toolkit*. Available at https://educationendow-mentfoundation.org.uk/evidence-summaries/teaching-learning-toolkit [Accessed 30 August 2019].

DfE (2013) *The National Curriculum in England Key Stages 1 and 2 Framework Document*. Available at https://assets.publishing.service.gov.uk/government/uploads/system/uploads/attachment_data/file/425601/PRIMARY_national_curriculum.pdf [Accessed 30 August 2019].

Fischer Family Trust (2018) *Reciprocal Reading*. Available at http://literacy.fischer-trust.org/overview/rr/ [Accessed 30 August 2019].

Kamler, B., and Thomson, P. (2008) The failure of dissertation advice books: Towards alternative pedagogies for doctoral writing. *Educational Researcher* Vol. 37, no. 8, pp. 507–518.

Kleine, D., Pearson, G., and Poveda, S. (2016) *Participatory Methods: Engaging Children's Voices and Experiences in Research*. Available at www.globalkidsonline.net/partici-patory-research [Accessed 30 August 2019].

Leat, D., and Reid, A. (2012) Exploring the role of student researchers in the process of curriculum development. *Curriculum Journal* Vol. 23, no. 2, pp. 189–205.

SAPERE (1992) *Philosophy for Children, Colleges, Communities*. Available at https://www.sapere.org.uk/ [Accessed 30 August 2019].

Chapter Seven

Young researchers in action

Kings Heath Primary School

Paul Clabon

Introduction

Kings Heath Primary School has been involved in the Young Researchers Project for five years. To begin with, higher-attaining children were chosen to take part in the project. However, more recently, children with a range of academic attainments have been chosen to take part. We have found that it is more important for children involved in the project to be keen and pro-active in their approach, rather than to be 'top of the class' academically.

Research questions

Our research projects are centred around topics that the children in our school will find meaningful to investigate. For example, recently we have looked at academisation as the school were considering joining a multi-academy trust (MAT) and also at the effectiveness of using online homework packages. There is a temptation to view the conference at the end of the project as a performance and to use this as an opportunity to showcase what is happening in our school, rather than to present an honest picture of the research we have been carrying out. This is why it is important to ask the children what they want the research project to focus on and to allow them to lead as many aspects of the work as possible. I meet with the young researchers regularly throughout the projects and allow them to take the lead in designing and carrying out the research.

Paul Clabon

Table 7.1 Research questions

Research questions
Is our new online homework worth the money we spend on it? Does it help children learn better than paper homework? Does homework for primary age children help them learn?

Our latest project looked at homework and how useful it was, as there was a concern in school that homework was not helping children's learning as much as we might want it to. For this project, our research questions are outlined in Table 7.1.

Previous research

Nicola worked with us as our research assistant on this project and sent the research digest shown in Table 7.2 to let the children know about previous research on the effectiveness of homework in primary schools. The references used for the research digest are provided at the end of this chapter.

Table 7.2 Research digest

1. What kind of research findings are there about homework in primary schools?

There has not been much research into homework in primary schools specifically. Most of the research about homework looks at secondary pupils. The Education Endowment Foundation have recently published a summary of some of the research into primary school homework. John Hattie also looked at lots of things that might affect how well children do in their school work and homework was one of these things. Nicholas Rudman is a primary school headteacher who carried out some PhD research into primary school homework and has published a summary of research that other people have written about in this area. I have used these three pieces of work to answer your other questions.

2. Does homework help children to learn?

The EEF say that, overall, homework does not appear to help primary children to learn very much. However, this is not a very strong finding as (a) there is not much research into primary school homework and (b) schools have very different approaches to homework so it is hard to compare them and see which might help children to learn best.

EEF and John Hattie both found that shorter, focussed tasks make better homework. John Hattie says that 5 to 10 minutes of homework has the same effect as one to two hours! He also says that the best homework is when you are practising something you have learned in school. The worst sort of homework to help you learn is a project based on something you have not been taught about yet in school. Nicholas Rudman found out that it is not a good idea to do your homework with the television on (yes, your parents and teachers are right about this one!). However, music can help some children to get their homework done, especially music with no words.

3. What do parents think about homework?

John Hattie and Nicholas Rudman both found that parents think that if schools give out homework, it shows that teachers are serious about the children learning. If a school does not give any homework, it can make parents think that they are not bothered about whether the children learn things or not, so they might not choose that school for their family. However, sometimes parents find that homework disrupts their family time and stops them doing other things with their children because there is not enough time.

All the research shows that parents need to support their children with homework at primary school age. However, Nicholas Rudman found out that sometimes parents getting involved is not a good thing, e.g. if the parent does not understand the homework properly or if they get cross with their child for not being able to do it, or for not finishing it quickly!

Parents can make a particularly big difference to their children's learning if they help them with reading at home. Nicholas Rudman found that the best way parents can help their children learn to read is to teach them specific things, like phonics. This is better than reading to children or listening to them read, if we want them to improve their reading. However, we also know that reading to or listening to children read is very important for developing a love of reading, so parents need to do this too.

4. What do children think about homework?

There is not much research about this at all. However, Nicholas Rudman did find that as children get older (towards secondary school age), they may get bored with homework, especially if their teachers do not give them any feedback about it. Secondary pupils like to choose when and where they do their homework, whereas primary pupils will usually be happy to do it where and when their parents tell them to.

5. Is there any (comparative) evidence about the effectiveness of online/computer based learning?

Again there is very little research that looks at online/computer based learning for primary children. For example, James Penner led a research team in the US looking at this, but from the point of view of college students. He found that there were no particular benefits of online homework versus 'pen and pencil' homework. Computer-based homework tended to be more structured, which meant that college students focussed on completing it as quickly as possible, rather than exploring ideas further. This might not be so important for primary school pupils, but college students need to explore ideas further to do well.

Other researchers have also looked at the advantages and disadvantages of online homework and found that it does not seem to make a difference either way. What is important is that teachers think about what work they are setting and whether it would benefit the children in their class to do it at home.

Methodology

We have used a number of different research methods in our projects, with varying degrees of success. When researching homework, we started with focus groups of children, to gain a broad idea of what children thought about the online homework. Next, we designed a questionnaire and tested it on a small sample of children. After this pilot, we made some changes to the questionnaire and then turned it into an online tool so that the results could be analysed more quickly. Use of an online tool enabled us to create graphs of the results, so that children could see the different responses to our questions very clearly. We altered the questionnaire slightly for parent participants. At our regular research meetings, we looked at how far we had come with the project and made decisions about what we needed to do next. So for example, after our initial data collection and analysis on the homework project from our parent and child questionnaires, we realised that children and their families were experiencing a lot of technical problems with completing their homework online. We also discussed who else we might need to talk to about our research. The children came up with the following list of actions for the coming weeks:

1. Finish off the parent questionnaire and analyse the results.
2. Try to find out more about the technical problems and whether they can be fixed.
3. Ask the teachers if they think homework helps learning and what they think about the new system.
4. Give the results to Ms McMichael and Ms Bowker because they are in charge of maths and English.
5. Give the results to Ms Hanson the headteacher because she is in charge of everything.

The Young Researchers Project has given us the opportunity to work with other schools in the city when carrying out our research. This is a useful way of children being able to explore situations beyond their own school context and gather data from a wider range of participants for their projects. For example, when looking at the issue of academisation, we decided to visit other schools to find out about their experiences of being part of a MAT. However, on reflection, this was less successful as a research method when working with the children on this particular project, as they tended to focus on superficial aspects of what they saw; for example, they were all very excited about the idea of having tablet computers and saw this as an advantage of being part of a MAT, as it was what they saw on their visit! For me, this visit highlighted the point that children involved in research projects will see things from their own particular point of view and tend to focus on the practical, 'day to day' aspects of school life, rather than always seeing the bigger educational or political picture.

Table 7.3 Research findings

Research findings
Children in our school think that homework helps them learn.
Children in our school think that primary schools should set homework.
Children in our school are more likely to do their homework now that it is online.
Children in our school do not enjoy homework more now that it is online.
Children in our school prefer to do their homework on paper.
Children report a lot of problems with getting on to the website to do their homework.

Findings

The findings from all of our research projects have been shared with teachers and governors at the school, with some influence on policy and practice at Kings Heath Primary School.

The key findings of the homework project are summarised in Table 7.3.

Having found that children and parents were experiencing a lot of technical difficulties in accessing the online homework, this led to a further investigation into the scale of these difficulties and how they might be resolved. It was a surprise to us that most children preferred paper homework and that children had found that they do not enjoy their homework more online. As a result of the project and further investigations, as a school we made the decision to continue with maths homework online but go back to spellings homework being on paper. We have also provided children and their families with more ideas about how to practise spellings at home.

Commentary

Children's voice at Kings Heath

The children at Kings Heath are clearly taking an active role in shaping their own lives and those of their classmates (James and Prout, 2015). Following their research into the effectiveness of online homework, the children were able to see that their research had made an impact on practice in school, resulting in a change in the homework policy. Kinney (2005) warns about the danger of working with a particular agenda in carrying out research with children. If the adults have already made assumptions about what story the research will tell, there is a risk that they only hear the information that relates to these assumptions. However, at Kings Heath it is clear that the adults involved in the Young Researchers Project are listening with intent to what their children are telling them. This is illustrated by the way that the young researchers' finding about the preference for paper homework was a surprise to their teachers. Here we see an example of young researchers using their project as more than a tool for investigating areas for development on a School Improvement Plan. Rather, they are using their collective voice to improve the lived experiences of all the children in the school, by drawing attention to the realities of completing homework online for children and their families. Furthermore, we can see that the children at Kings Heath have an expectation that their research will be listened to, in their decision to communicate their findings to the English and mathematics leads and to their headteacher, 'because she is in charge of everything'. These young researchers have the confidence to take their findings to the people who they know are in a position to make decisions.

The earlier research project on academisation raised some challenges for the research assistant involved. As Qvortrup (2015) points out, the interests of adults are not always the same as those of children, even when we are looking at parents and their own children, or teachers and the children in their schools. The issue of academisation is potentially problematic, involving both local and national politics. The children had asked to look into academisation as they knew that this was a possibility for their school. Many of the parents at Kings Heath Primary were opposed to the idea of the school becoming an academy and had been quite vocal in their opposition. When asked to carry out a literature search, the research assistant was quite concerned about how the contents of the research digest might affect the children. Academisation has the potential to be an emotional issue for parents and thus for children and it was important to consider how carrying out this project might create or heighten any anxieties that the children might have. On the one hand, both teachers and academics involved in the Young Researchers Project are committed to the notion that research can be used to allow children to engage in democratic practice. Furthermore, this can sometimes give them the opportunity to challenge adults' thinking and decision making (Kinney, 2005). On the other hand, as Veale (2006) points out, if children are not the ones who have the ultimate control of resources, it may be unfair to allow them to carry out research into areas such as academisation. There was a concern amongst the adults involved in this project that allowing children to research the effectiveness of academisation could raise an expectation of influence on the final decision that may not be fulfilled. There was a possibility that being involved in the Young Researchers Project could create anxieties for these children around academisation that might not be visible if this was an issue that was discussed and decided on by adults. It was important to reflect on this, but as Qvortrup (2015) points out, the desire to protect children can lead to them being excluded from discussions and decisions that have an impact on their everyday lives. So in this case, the research was undertaken on the basis that children needed to be included in those discussions, rather than just overhearing them at home and at school. Although they may not have been able to have a direct influence on the decision that was to be made, the Young Researchers Project allowed the children's voices to be heard and for a decision to be made with full knowledge of how children might feel about and react to the practical consequences of that decision. In reality, once children were involved in the project, it was noticeable that, beyond rehearsing what they had heard their parents talking about at home, they were not so interested in engaging with the political agenda around academisation. Instead, the children focused on the practicalities of the possible change. For example, one of the questions they asked was, 'What opportunities and benefits might there be to sharing facilities between schools in a MAT?' So in this project, children demonstrated that they are capable of defining and shaping their own realities and following their own agenda in research, rather than having an agenda forced on them, albeit unintentionally, by adults. Rather than creating anxieties for the children, the project allowed them to speak about the aspects of academisation that they were concerned with and that would impact on their own day to day experiences.

Children's participation at Kings Heath

In considering Kleine et al.'s (2016) principle of **relevance**, the children at Kings Heath have shown us that it is not up to adults to decide what are relevant topics of research for young children. The young researchers in this case study demonstrate that children will make research relevant to their own lives and to the lives of the children around them. The adults involved in the academisation research had concerns that needed to be reflected on in terms of their responsibility towards the children. However, the young researchers showed that if a space for their voice is opened up, they will use that space to define their own interests and to shape the direction of the research project. Similarly, when investigating the effectiveness of the schools' homework policy, the children's analysis of the findings allowed them to challenge adults' thinking in relation to what kinds of homework were most motivating for the children. By recognising the children's knowledge in relation to homework and making changes to practices and policy in school, the adults involved demonstrated the principle of **empowerment.** We have already discussed that empowerment is a tricky term in relation to young researchers, as it can suggest that adults hold all the power and decide to hand some over to children. However, this case study demonstrates that empowerment can be seen as a more reciprocal and collaborative principle, where the knowledge and power moves between the parties involved. In this case study, it can be argued that the children's findings empowered the adults to make decisions that would improve the lives and learning of the whole of the school community.

References

Education Endowment Foundation (2018) *Homework (Primary).* Available at https:// educationendowmentfoundation.org.uk/evidence-summaries/teaching-learning-toolkit/homework-primary/ [Accessed 30 August 2019].

Hattie, J. A. C. (2009) *Visible Learning: A Synthesis of Over 800 Meta-analyses Relating to Achievement.* Routledge: Abingdon.

James, A., and Prout, A. (2015) *Constructing and Reconstructing Childhood: Contemporary Issues in the Sociological Study of Childhood.* Routledge: Abingdon.

Kinney, L. (2005) Small voices … Powerful messages in Clark, A., Kjorholt, A. T. and Moss, P. (eds.) *Beyond Listening: Children's Perspectives on Early Childhood Services.* Policy Press: Bristol.

Kleine, D., Pearson, G., and Poveda, S. (2016) *Participatory Methods: Engaging Children's Voices and Experiences in Research.* Available at www.globalkidsonline.net/partici-patory-research [Accessed 30 August 2019].

Penner, J., Kreuze, E., Langsam S., and Kreuze, J. (2016) *Online Homework Versus Pen and Pencil Homework: Do the Benefits Outweigh the Costs?* Available at http:// www.wiu.edu/cbt/jcbi/documents/NAASFeb2016/SpecialNAASIssueFeb2016-OnlineHomeworkVsPenAndPencilHomework.pdf [Accessed 30 August 2019].

Qvortrup, J. (2015) A Voice for Children in Statistical and Social Accounting: A Plea for Children's Right to Be Heard. In: James, A. and Prout, A. (eds.) *Constructing and Reconstructing Childhood: Contemporary Issues in the Sociological Study of Childhood.* Routledge: Abingdon.

Rudman, N. (2014a) A Review of Homework Literature as a Precursor to Practitioner-Led Doctoral Research in a Primary School. *Research in Education.* Vol. 91, no. 1, pp. 12–29.

Rudman, N. (2014b) *Conceptualising Homework in an Essex Primary School: Learning from Our Community*. Available at https://ethos.bl.uk/OrderDetails.do;jsessionid =0CCA11218D00AF3D891264DCCC30A4BC?uin=uk.bl.ethos.669002 [Accessed 30 August 2019].

Veale, A. (2006) Creative Methodologies in Participatory Research with Children. In: Greene, S. and Hogan, D. (eds.) *Researching Children's Experience: Approaches and Methods*. Sage: London.

Chapter Eight

Young researchers in action

Cockshut Hill School

Steven Moore

Introduction

Cockshut Hill School became part of Summit Learning Trust in 2016. It is an average-sized secondary school, with just over one thousand Year 7 to 11 pupils. The proportion of pupils eligible for Pupil Premium is well above average and the proportion of SEN pupils is also above average. Approximately half of pupils are from an ethnic minority background with the biggest proportion of these being Pakistani. The number of pupils with English as an additional language is also above average at around 50%. The school also has a large number of pupils who join the school during the school year.

2018 was the first time Cockshut Hill took part in the Young Researchers Project and as the member of staff in charge of Pupil Voice in school, it seemed a natural fit for me to lead the project. I had around 15 years' experience as a class-room teacher, ten years of which I have spent either seconded to or sitting on the Senior Leadership Team. Having a senior leader working on the project afforded the opportunity to consistently have a platform on which to make decisions and communicate to staff.

The newly elected pupil leadership group consisting of 12 house leaders had spent the autumn term working on a Pupil School Improvement Plan. This entailed them using the School Improvement Plan and communicating how pupils could help the school realise the priorities outlined within it. A large part of the plan was focused on teaching and learning, so I took the opportunity to launch the Young Researchers Project as a vehicle for pupils driving change in teaching and learning in school. All pupils from Key Stage Three were invited to apply for a place as a Young Researcher outlining why they would be a suitable candidate in a single paragraph. The idea of this was to try to add kudos to the position as well as to get pupils to reflect on what skills they could bring to the project. It also had pupils doing something in their own time straight away. The expectation that they would be undertaking work was immediately in place.

Research questions

Eight pupils were chosen on the strength of their application paragraphs; two were from Year 7, three from Year 8 and three from Year 9. These young researchers were from a variety of previous attainment and ethnic groups. After the official University Day, where they learnt about the kinds of activities they would be undertaking, the pupils took the pupil school improvement plan and were given free reign as to what element of teaching and learning they were going to explore. School priorities married up to five of the six principles identified within Making Every Lesson Count (Tharby and Allison, 2015) and of those five principles the young researchers chose to investigate modelling in lessons. They were given a copy of the book and had two weeks to read the chapter on effective modelling in lessons. Pupils were aware at the launch stage that there would be the requirement for them to try and access academic literature and this was the first time for some that they had read a non-fiction book aimed at adults.

After two weeks every pupil returned with annotated chapters to varying degrees. Pupils could all communicate what they believed modelling was and could share their own experiences of what they had experienced in school so far. Pupils were in agreement over the importance of modelling but there was conjecture around what they thought about their experiences of modelling at school was. From this discussion the pupils decided their question would be:

How effective is modelling at Cockshut Hill School?

In order to answer the overriding investigation question the pupils came up with a series of questions they would answer, outlined in Table 8.1

Table 8.1 Research questions

Research questions
What is modelling?
What types of modelling happen at Cockshut Hill?
Is modelling consistent?
What advice can we give to improve modelling?
Can we learn better modelling from primary education?

Previous research

We met on a weekly basis from this point onwards during a 30-minute form period at the beginning of the school day. The key points from Tharby and Allison (2015) in relation to modelling were:

- Modelling demonstrates the high standard expected of a particular task.
- Modelling can be useful to demonstrate expected behaviours as well as how to complete particular tasks.
- Modelling is most effective when broken down into a sequence of steps.
- Live modelling is useful to demonstrate a process that you want children to understand.
- Modelling can help to demonstrate the struggle involved in completing a task.
- Talk by the teacher and between teacher and pupils is an important element of modelling.
- Children's work can also be used as an effective model.
- Modelling common errors and how to address them can be useful

The next step was to broaden the research into modelling and research techniques in general. Pupils were given academic journals to read and discuss. Whilst all had accessed the book, journals proved too complicated for some. In an attempt to negate these difficulties, we watched video clips based around the ideas outlined in the journals, for example a clip that explains Bandura's Social Learning Theory (The Curious Classroom, 2013). This proved to be a very successful method of getting all pupils to understand what they were looking for as well as wider approaches to research. Pupils could verbalise what they thought of Bandura's Social Learning Theory and Vygotsky's Social Constructivist Theory having previously floundered when reading about them.

Methodology

As a geography specialist, I have a lot of experience teaching about data collection. We spent some of our sessions learning about qualitative and quantitative data – the value and limitations of each as well as discussing techniques. As part of my role across school I complete a termly pupil questionnaire to one third of the pupil body so this presented a good opportunity for the pupils to get a large amount of responses about pupil impressions on modelling in school. Pupils decided they wanted to observe lessons first hand and experience what was happening in classrooms other than their own. At the time teaching and learning was monitored by staff over three windows in the school calendar called teaching and learning review weeks. During these weeks there are a lot of observations and learning walks conducted around school. The pupils used this opportunity to visit lessons subjects of their choosing around school in pairs. As part of these observations, the researchers also spoke to pupils in lessons and looked at books. Each pair visited 4 different lessons meaning 16 lessons were visited in total. Where possible, researchers were kept away from their own year group's lessons as they felt it might be disruptive to see close peers when undertaking the research. Teachers were consulted ahead of the observations and knew which pupils to expect and the focus of the observation. Researchers were briefed to focus on modelling and were given a rough time span of about 20 minutes to spend in the lessons. They were allowed to have discussions with pupils in the lessons as long as they did not disrupt the teacher's delivery, much like any member of staff undertaking a classroom observation. Feedback from the teachers who were being observed praised the young researchers' mature approach and at times took the opportunity to engage them in reverse coaching conversations. Each pair was then tasked with presenting what they had found to their fellow researchers. Yardley Wood Primary School welcomed the researchers in to observe lessons in their school to identify comparisons with modelling in the primary environment.

Findings

The researchers observed elements of modelling in all 16 of the lessons they visited at Cockshut Hill as well as all eight lessons at Yardley Wood. They concluded that modelling was particularly useful in practical subjects such as PE, science and art. They noticed that using pupils to model ideas helped with engagement and were very positive about the idea of pupils taking an active role in modelling.

The most effective modelling often involved pupils answering questions as an idea was modelled. Some researchers noted that teachers were using questioning to draw out pupils' ideas and in doing so model for other pupils what they should do. The young researchers noticed that this helped with engagement and also allowed misconceptions to be addressed immediately. The use of real-world examples in maths and art encouraged the researchers to consider how modelling could be more effective when placed into a context. The researchers noticed that tablet computers and visualisers were useful tools for modelling in lessons. Presentation software like PowerPoint or Keynote was used regularly in lessons and the researchers recognised the clear potential of it in modelling terms. However, they noticed that if there was too much information, particularly text, this could be difficult for pupils to follow. Researchers preferred it when minimal writing was used and teachers took the opportunity to display little and explain more. Their observation notes showed that reading from slides as pupils were looking at them could be confusing and make the modelling hard to follow. The live modelling of pictorial or literary annotation was suggested as the most effective way to utilise these presentations.

From the primary school visit, the group felt there were two areas that stood out in terms of practice they felt were beneficial in addition to what they had seen in our school. First, there were a lot more teachers or teaching assistants in lessons. They noted this enabled modelling of the same thing in slightly different ways and felt this afforded pupils more chance to understand concepts. Second, they identified display as being a useful tool to model to pupils. The visual prompts around the room were not seen to be as explicitly referred to in our school.

The young researchers presented their projects to the whole staff body in a staff briefing. They outlined work they had done, theory they had studied and their chief findings. At the end of the briefing each member of teaching staff and teaching assistants made a pledge to improve their practice in some way. Where the researchers explicitly referenced subjects in their feedback, staff aimed to follow their advice. Where subjects hadn't been referred to it was clear staff had reflected on the more general points they had made.

Reflection

As a teacher I feel the Young Researchers Project presented the opportunity to hear the views of the most important stakeholders in the school on the diet of pedagogy they were receiving. I felt that the whole staff body bought into what they were advising as a result of their research findings. To hear directly from the pupils you are teaching about what they perceive to be going on in the classroom is perhaps more of a powerful tool than hearing from a colleague. I believe that making it explicit to staff that the young researchers' views had a grounding in academic research potentially added credence to their messages.

I was surprised at the buy-in from the pupils involved. Possibly requiring pupils to apply for the position helped with this, but, even so, scheduled weekly meetings and reading in their own time meant it was a significant undertaking for pupils. As stated earlier, this was a mixed age and attainment group but this did not deter them from reading published work aimed at adults and then demonstrating enough comprehension to discuss what they had understood.

We currently operate a model of pupil leadership that involves six broad pupil groups. The researchers have all joined these groups and maintain prominence in the pupil body. At the time of writing most have discussed future positions in the highest echelons of pupil leadership in school. In terms of the legacy of the project, a year later modelling remains a focus in our teaching and learning principles. I am regularly invited to see colleagues demonstrating modelling in their lessons with specific reference to the findings of the research project.

Commentary

Children's voice at Cockshut Hill

As with the other case studies in this book, we can see that at Cockshut Hill, the Young Researchers Project opened up a space for the children's voices to be heard. In this particular project, the adults involved took a brave decision to allow children to explore an aspect of teaching and learning, which, as discussed below, has the potential to be threatening for teachers. We know that working as researchers gives children an opportunity to let us know about how they see their worlds and that young researchers can be an effective channel of communication for their peers (Kerawalla and Messer, 2019). We also know that engaging with rigorous research methods can be a challenge for children (Bradbury-Jones and Taylor, 2015). The Young Researchers Project demonstrates that children can do this whilst operating effectively in the largely adult space of research methodology. Children in this project were able to generate new knowledge about modelling, by merging their understanding of the academic literature with their knowledge of what was happening in their classrooms (Veale, 2006). Importantly, their findings were then listened to and acted upon by their teachers. We know from previous work with children as researchers that there can be a tendency for children's findings to be forgotten (Alderson, 2017). However, in this project adults were open to listening to children and to making changes to what happened in their classrooms in response to the project's findings. As with many of the projects carried out in our schools, this work on modelling was linked to the school improvement plan. This could be seen as putting constraints on what children can research and meaning that they are being forced to research according to the agenda of adults. However, we would argue that children in school are already constrained by the fact that, in our society, they have to attend school. Once in school, children are constrained by rules and regulations that govern their time in school: timetables, uniform, rewards and sanctions for behaviour, etc. Within this environment, allowing children some influence over such an important document as a school improvement plan demonstrates a real commitment to creating a space for children's voices to be heard and listened to with intent. Adults are less likely to dismiss children's contributions if they are focused on a joint endeavour, such as a school improvement plan. In this study, as Steven highlights, the children's clear understanding of the research literature gave real strength to their voice in relation to teaching and learning.

Children's participation at Cockshut Hill

This case study particularly reflects Kleine et al.'s (2016) principles of **relevance**, **empowerment** and **flexibility**. Although the children involved were constrained in their choice of research topic by the school development plan, they were able to research an area of direct relevance to their own learning i.e. modelling. They were able to participate in research carried out in a similar way to that undertaken by adult researchers, by reading relevant literature and thinking about how their understanding of this reading linked to what they were observing in the classroom. Children made this research relevant to their own experiences by focussing on what was most useful in relation to children's learning. They also demonstrated that they were able to analyse their data by making comparisons between different contexts and drawing out the relevance of the primary school experience for their own secondary classrooms.

The issue of empowerment in relation to participation is potentially a difficult one in relation to this research study. As Alderson (2017) asserts, adults can feel threatened by research involving children's participation and in the case of teacher/pupil relationships, this could be particularly problematic. Not all teachers would be comfortable with allowing their pupils to observe and comment on what is happening in their classrooms. There is also the argument that children are not experts in teaching and so should not be asked to make judgements on how effective qualified and experienced teachers are in aspects of their teaching. We have previous discussed the notion of power in relation to children's research and it could be argued that in this research project, the balance of power could tip too far in the direction of the children. This is where it is important to remember that young researchers' projects are about children being given the opportunity to define their own realities (Veale, 2006) and to take an active role in shaping their own lives and those of others in their school community. Thus this research was carried out with the full support of teachers, as the young researchers were exploring the lived experiences of their classmates in terms of how modelling helped their learning, rather than making judgements about teacher effectiveness.

The danger with Young Researchers Projects such as this one is that they can become a tool for school improvement with a focus on individuals' teaching practice, rather than a means by which children can be given an opportunity to show what their lived experience in school is and how this might be made better. We would recommend that if a project is going to involve classroom observation, it must be made very clear from the start that researchers are observing how children experience what is happening in the classroom and not making comments or judgements on what the teacher is doing. This can only happen effectively and without any negative impact on teachers if observation as a means of sharing practice is embedded in the culture of the school.

In this project, Steven demonstrated flexibility by responding to the challenges that arose as the work developed, for example by using video to help the children access some of the more challenging literature. Alderson (2017) highlights the way in which over complication of research terms can be a barrier to children participating in a meaningful way in research projects. This barrier is first addressed in the Young Researchers Project at the University Day, as discussed in Chapter 4. The idea of academics acting as research assistants for the projects is also designed to overcome this challenge in researching with young children. However, in the case of the young researchers at Cockshut Hill, the children shaped their research design in a different way, by undertaking the reading themselves. Steven could have responded to their difficulty with accessing some of the texts by following the established pattern of requesting a research digest from Debbie and Nicola. However, instead he found a way of addressing this challenge that allowed the children to still be in control of this aspect of the research project. In this sense, he demonstrated flexibility whilst still remaining committed to the principle of children taking the lead in shaping their young researchers project.

References

Alderson, P. (2017) Children as researchers: the effects of participation rights on research methodology. In: Christensen, P. & James, A. (eds.), *Research with children: Practices and perspectives*. Routledge: Abingdon.

Bradbury-Jones, C. & Taylor, J. (2015) Engaging with children as co-researchers: challenges, counter-challenges and solutions, *International Journal of Social Research Methodology* Vol. 18, no. 2, pp. 161–173.

Kerawalla, L and Messer, D (2019). Is being a young researcher always a positive learning experience? *Interdisciplinary Education and Psychology* Vol. 2, no. 2. Available at http://riverapublications.com/article/is-being-a-young-researcher-always-a-positive-learning-experience [Accessed 05 August 2020].

Kleine, D., Pearson, G., & Poveda, S. (2016) *Participatory methods: Engaging children's voices and experiences in research*. Available at www.globalkidsonline.net/participatory-research [Accessed 30 August 2019].

Tharby, A. & Allison, S. (2015) *Making every lesson count: Six principles to support great teaching and learning*. Crown House Publishing Ltd.: Carmarthen.

The Curious Classroom (2013) *Bandura and social learning theory*. Available at https://www.youtube.com/watch?v=NjTxQy_U3ac [Accessed 30 August 2019].

Veale, A. (2006) Creative Methodologies in Participatory Research with Children. In: Greene, S. & Hogan, D. (eds.), *Researching children's experience: Approaches and methods*. Sage: London.

Chapter Nine

Your own Young Researchers Project

Debbie Reel and Nicola Smith

Introduction

This chapter is designed to support teachers who would like to work on their own projects with children as researchers. It will outline the role of the adult in such a research project; how to decide on your research team and organise your meetings; how to decide on the research focus and plan the research questions. Aspects of methodology will be explored; namely the use of questionnaires/surveys, interviews and observations. Some of the ethical issues that may arise in projects are discussed. There is support for collecting and analysing data and for presenting your findings. We also include some more detail on our presentation from the University Day, for use in training teachers and young researchers.

The role of the adult in the Young Researchers Project

As a teacher working on a young researchers project, it is important to remember that you are in a supportive, facilitative role, rather than one of leading the project. You need to be confident in your understanding of how to carry out research, so you may need to read up on research methods if it has been a while since you carried out any research of your own, e.g. for a university dissertation. Some useful texts are included at the end of this chapter. You may also wish to arrange to work in partnership with a higher education provider, so that you can be supported as you work with the children on the project. You will need to be given time to work on the project, so that you can carry out the following aspects of your role:

- Organising meetings, including times and places
- Supporting children with administrative aspects of the project e.g. photocopying and printing
- Supporting children to work as a team
- Recognising and pointing out any potential pitfalls with the children's chosen research focus or research methods
- Prompting children to make sure that they keep their focus on their role as young researchers
- Technical support, e.g. for recording interviews and/or observations.

A template for a research plan is included in Figure 9.1.

Deciding on your research team

Although, in an ideal world, any pupil who would like to be a member of a young researchers' team should be given the opportunity, this is not usually achievable because of practical and methodological limitations. Most of our participating schools operated some sort of selection procedure for their young researchers. It is important that this procedure is clear and transparent for the children. So, for example, if you are going to ask for letters of application, then you need to make the criteria for selection clear to the children before they apply. An example is included in Figure 9.2.

Young children will also need help to think about how they can show that they are good at doing these things. You may also want to consider whether written applications are the fairest way to begin the selection procedure. It might be better to invite anyone interested to come along to an introductory meeting to hear about what the project involves. Then, any interested children could attend an informal interview. It is important that children understand that being a young researcher is about finding out what other people are doing and thinking. It is not about being able to have their own ideas listened to as a priority over others. You will need to think carefully about how you are going to let children know whether they have been successful in their applications as this needs to be communicated in a sensitive manner. It is helpful to stress to children that they can participate in the projects in other ways if they are not a researcher (by participating in any interviews, focus groups or questionnaires, for example), and that this is a way in which they can communicate their ideas and have their voice heard.

Title of Research Project:

Names of Young Researchers	
Names of Young Researchers Adult in School	
Name and contact details of Research Assistant	
Dates and times of YRP meetings	
Research question/s	

Research methods: data collection	Method	Dates for completion

Research methods: data analysis	Tasks to complete	Dates for completion

Reporting the research findings	Date to complete research report	
	Date of YRP conference	
	Date of presentation to governors	
	Date of presentation to pupils and parents	

Figure 9.1: Research plan

Title of Research Project: Teaching and Learning x tables effectively.

Names of Young Researchers	L.R, E.G, R.b, K.T, H.R.
Names of Young Researchers Adult in School	Mrs Johnson.
Name and contact details of Research Assistant	Debbie Reel.
Dates and times of YRP meetings	Oct 2019 Feb 2020 Nov 2019 March 2020 Dec 2020 May 2020 Jan 2020 (lunch-times).
Research question/s	How effective is the teaching of x tables in our yr 4 classes?

Research methods: data collection	Method	Dates for completion
	Questionnaires (Children)	Feb 2020
	Interviews (Staff).	April 2020.

Research methods: data analysis	Tasks to complete	Dates for completion
	Look for key themes in questionnaires and interviews and draw conclusions.	March 2020. May 2020.

Reporting the research findings	Date to complete research report
	beg June 2020.
	Date of YRP conference
	11th June 2020
	Date of presentation to governors
	end of June 2020
	Date of presentation to pupils and parents
	July 2020.

Figure 9.1: (*Continued*)

Do you want to be a young researcher? We are looking for people who can:

1. Show commitment to coming to young researchers meetings
2. Work well in a small team e.g. take turns; help others;
3. Listen carefully to other children
4. Communicate their ideas to other children and adults
5. Help to make things better in our school for all pupils

Figure 9.2: Criteria for young researcher applications

Organising your research team meetings

Regular meetings help to keep children's interest in the project and maintain momentum, as well as ensuring that children remember what stage of the project they are at. Ideally, you should meet with your group of young researchers on a fortnightly basis for at least half an hour. All of our young researchers enjoy having the identity of being a researcher and some of the groups have special notebooks and/or badges to emphasise this. Biscuits are a very popular feature of young researchers meetings in several of our schools! At the first meeting, you might want to explain exactly what will be involved in being a young researcher and allow time for any questions that the children might have. It is helpful to have a plan for each meeting – this could be based on the research plan template included in Figure 9.1. Remember that the young researchers need to lead the project as much as possible, so they may want to decide on different roles for each person, or they may decide to take turns, e.g. at being the chairperson or note taker for each meeting. Some groups find it helpful to draw up a set of agreed 'ground rules' for how young researchers will behave in meetings.

Deciding on the research focus

As discussed in our case study chapters, often a research focus will be linked to the school development plan. Although, in an ideal world, children would have a completely free choice of research topic, if you are going to provide this opportunity you need to think through the implications very carefully. We would argue that it is better for children to focus on an area in the school development plan if this gives their research findings a higher likelihood of having an impact on practice in school. If children are given a completely free choice of research focus, you may find yourself in a situation where you do not have the funds, time or other resources to act in a meaningful way on their research findings.

Within your group of young researchers, you may have children with different priorities or opinions about what the research focus should be. In this case, you need to make sure that children listen to each other's points of view before making a decision, perhaps by having a formal vote. However the children decide on the research focus, you need to support them to consider if their research will be manageable in the given time for the project. You also need to make sure that children are clear about exactly what they want to find out, so that they can plan meaningful research questions.

Planning the research questions

To begin with, children might come up with all the questions that they have about a particular topic. This can be useful, but children may find it difficult to decide on a particular focus for their research. Sue Bucknall's (2012) suggestion of referring to 'big' and 'little' questions is useful here. The 'big' question is the overall research question, whereas the 'little' questions are those that can be used to collect data, which will be analysed with the aim of answering the 'big' research question. For example, at Cockshut Hill School in Chapter 8, the 'big' research question was, 'How effective is modelling at Cockshut Hill School?' The 'little' research questions were:

- What is modelling?
- What types of modelling happen at Cockshut Hill?
- Is modelling consistent?
- What advice can we give to improve modelling?

Selecting research methods

Once the children have decided on their research questions, they need to think about what the most suitable methods are for collecting their data. For our children, this is where the University Day and regular meetings with the Young Researchers Project leaders provides support for the children in developing their research skills. You will need to think about how you might provide this support or training for your young researchers. You may decide to partner with a local university in working on your projects or you may access one of the publications available to help you provide your own training, such as this book or one of the others listed in 'Useful sources of further support and information' at the end of this chapter. Our young researchers have used one of, or a combination of three data collection methods:

* Questionnaire
* Interview
* Observation.

It is important to state that other research methods are used by researchers, such as experiments, for example, but to date these have not been appropriate for the particular projects carried out by our young researchers. You will need to discuss the advantages and disadvantages of each method with your group of young researchers so that they can come to a decision about the most appropriate method/s.

Questionnaire/survey

Almost all of our young researchers have used some sort of questionnaire or survey in their projects. This is because a questionnaire/survey allows you to access a larger number of research participants than other methods. They are also less time-consuming in terms of data collection as you do not have to remain with the participant as they answer the questions. However, questionnaires and surveys are only useful if the questions are carefully planned to ensure that you gather the information you need. For this reason, it is good practice, as with all research methods, to carry out a small pilot of your questionnaire/survey first. Send out five or six questionnaires to a representative sample of people of your group of participants and look at their responses carefully. Did you find out everything you needed to and if not, why not? Are there some questions missing? Or are some of your questions badly worded? The guidance that we provide to our schools on writing questionnaires is included in Figure 9.3.

Interviews

Children enjoy carrying out interviews, so you need to explain to them that they need to select the best method for their particular study, rather than the one that is the most fun! In research, there are two types of interviews; structured and semi-structured. In a

1. Keep everything short. Ideally your questionnaire should fit on one side of A4. Keep your questions clear and short too.

2. Only ask for one piece of information in each question.

3. Be very precise e.g. instead of just saying "How long do you spend on homework every week?" , give a choice e.g. One hour or less/One-two hours/Two-three hours

4. Plan carefully to make sure you collect all the necessary details. Try your questionnaire out as a pilot, in case you think, "Oh, I wish we had asked about ….."

5. Remember that most people want to look good and this might affect how they answer your questions. Try not to ask leading questions. For example, if you ask, "Do you think homework is important?" nearly everyone will say 'yes' because they are answering questions in school and do not want to look as if they are not working hard! Instead you could give them other things that you might do at home e.g. homework, spending time with family, taking part in sports etc and ask them to put them in order of importance.

Based on Thomas, G. (2013) *How to do your research project* Sage: London.

Figure 9.3: How to write a good questionnaire

structured interview, the questions are closed, which can mean that you can be more sure of obtaining the precise information you need. On the other hand, there is little opportunity for participants to tell you about their own feelings and opinions, particularly in relation to ideas that you may not have considered when planning your interview. Semi-structured interviews include more open questions, to allow participants to expand on their responses and opinions. This can give you more of a detailed insight into your particular area of enquiry. However, it can mean that you have lots of data to analyse, which can become unmanageable.

Both types of interview can be time-consuming, as you need at least 30 minutes with each participant in order to carry out a useful interview. This means that you can only carry out interviews with a few participants. Our young researchers have found interviews useful when they want to gain the views of headteachers or senior leaders, or if they want to speak to a few of their peers to gain more detailed insights after carrying out questionnaires.

If your young researchers are going to carry out interviews, we recommend that they voice record the interviews. It is almost impossible to write down every word of an interviewee's response as they are speaking. Voice recordings also mean that you can share the interviews with all the young researchers and listen to them together once you get to the data analysis stage. Your young researchers can practise interviewing one another first, so that they can make sure they are confident in reading out the planned questions. They can also practise being good listeners, e.g. making eye contact with the person they are interviewing. They will need to prepare a short explanation of the research project to share with participants at the beginning of the interview. It is also good practice to remember to thank your interviewee at the end of the process!

Observations

If your young researchers decide to carry out observations of teachers and/or children, there are a number of important points to consider. First, permission needs to be obtained from the headteacher, teacher, children and their parents for the observation to be carried out. If the young researchers are going to film their observations, they will need specific permission for this. They will need to provide information about how the films will be stored and for how long and who will be allowed to view them, and for what purpose.

Before carrying out an observation, it is important to think about exactly what you want to observe. For example, at Cockshut Hill, our young researchers knew that they wanted to observe how students responded to teacher modelling in lessons. This allowed them to plan out which lessons they would visit and to talk to the teachers about when would be the best time to carry out the observations. They could then plan questions to support their observation focus. Two examples of observation schedules that you might use are included in Figures 9.4 and 9.5.

Questions, questions …

In questionnaires, surveys and interviews, your young researchers will need to be skilled at asking questions. In research, it is as important to think about how you ask your questions as it is to think about what those questions are about. Children will need to understand what a 'leading question' is and how they can avoid these so that their research is not biased. You can practise this with children by providing some examples of 'leading questions' and more appropriate questions and sorting them

Title of Research Project:

Date of observation	
Name/s of observers	
Start/End time of observation	
Focus of observation	

Time	Observation Notes	Comments/analysis

Figure 9.4: Observation schedule 1

Title of Research Project:

Date of observation	14.2.2019	
Name/s of observers	Kayla, Ali	
Start/End time of observation	12.30pm - 1pm	
Focus of observation	Pupil tracking outdoors	
Time	Observation Notes	Comments/analysis
12.30pm	On bike, playing with A, delivering pizzas.	Friends Talking Exercise
12.38pm	Running around, chasing A + B	Friends Exercise ? Talking
12.42pm	Sitting on bench with A, talking.	Friends Talking
12.50pm	Talking to teacher, goes indoors	Talking
12.56pm	Comes out. Walking around	Exercise ? Looking for Friends

Figure 9.4: (*Continued*)

Title of Research Project

Date of observation	
Name/s of observers	
Start/End time of observation	
Focus of observation	

Behaviour observed	Frequency (Tally)	Total (Number)

Figure 9.5: Observation schedule 2

Title of Research Project

Date of observation	11.2.2019	
Name/s of observers	Claire, Ethan, Kayla, Ali	
Start/End time of observation	10:45 am - 11:05 am	
Focus of observation	Use of outdoor area - turns	
Behaviour observed	Frequency (Tally)	Total (Number)
Bikes - 1 seat	⊞ ⊞ ⊞	15
Bikes - 2 seat	IIII	4
Bench	II	2
Scooter	⊞ ⊞ III	13
Skipping Ropes	III	3
Hoops	II	2
Stilts	⊞ I	6
No equipment	⊞ III	8

We counted every time someone started playing with a piece of equipment

Figure 9.5: (*Continued*)

Table 9.1 Developing effective questions

Types of questions to avoid	What to ask instead
Those with a clear yes/no answer – focussing on only one option. **Does our school support regular outdoor activity?**	Create questions that allow children to debate a range of results and create an argument. **What can our school do to protect regular outdoor activity?**
One that is highly contentious or heavily loaded. **Why do boys prefer playing football to girls?**	Choose questions that are not presumptuous. **How can we make more time in the curriculum for a wide range of sports to be accessed by all?**
Too broad/impossible to answer. **Do all children in our city use too much single use plastic?**	Narrow your questions to allow for more specific answers. **How can our school contribute to limiting the use of 'single use' plastic?**
Too objective. **How much time do children spend playing per day?**	Think more about the subjective nature to a question and the relationship between that which you are researching and other factors. **What is the relationship between more time playing and children's wellbeing?**

with the children before discussion. Some examples of ineffective and more appropriate questions are provided in Table 9.1

Thinking about ethics

Bias is one aspect of ethical issues in research but there are others to consider as well. If you are a teacher, you will know that most children have a strong sense of what is 'fair' and what is not. We have found that this helps them to understand some of the ethical principles involved in carrying out research. So, for example, at the University Day we discuss the need to be fair to all participants by making sure that they understand what the research is about, how their information will be used and how the research findings will be shared at the end of the project. We also talk to the children about the importance of confidentiality and anonymity. This is communicated to the children as part of their responsibility as young researchers and we find that they take this aspect of their role very seriously. Other ethical principles include:

• The right of participants to withdraw from the research at any time
• The importance of keeping interview and questionnaire/survey questions clear and easy to understand

- Always asking permission before recording any interviews or observations
- Avoiding influencing responses, e.g. no leading questions; do not interview your best friends!
- Keep research participants informed about how the research project is progressing.

Collecting data

Collecting data is the exciting part of the research project and adult and children researchers alike are often keen to get started on this as soon as possible! However, it is important not to rush into this stage of the research if you want your data to be as useful as possible for your study. Before your young researchers begin collecting data, you need to make sure that they have:

1. Defined clear research questions
2. Selected appropriate research methods
3. Designed clear questionnaire/interview/survey/observation schedules
4. Piloted their questionnaire/survey/interview/observation
5. Planned how they will record and organise their data as they collect it.

Collating and organising data is an important aspect of the research project. Any researcher knows that it is all too easy to become overwhelmed with recordings and pieces of paper during the data collection stage of a project. Your young researchers will need to make sure that for every questionnaire, survey, interview or observation they carry out, the following information is clearly recorded:

- Date
- Name of participant (if using pseudonyms at this stage for confidentiality, how will you remember who is who, e.g. teacher/child in Year 1?)
- Name of interviewer/observer, if relevant.

It is also useful if researchers log any useful comments immediately after an interview or observation, e.g. 'interview with headteacher interrupted by phone call at 10.30 am'. We have provided a template that you might find useful for organising your data, for example from an interview, in Figure 9.6.

Title of Research Project:

Name of interviewer(s)	
Name of interviewee	
Pseudonym	
Date of interview	
Interviewer comments	
Data analysis date	
Data analysis notes	

Figure 9.6: Organising data-interview log

Title of Research Project: Outdoor Play in KS2.

Name of interviewer(s)	KS2 Young Researchers.
Name of interviewee	Mr Gregshaw
Pseudonym	—
Date of interview	January 12th 2020.
Interviewer comments	Mr Gregshaw, head of KS2, was interviewed. 6 questions were asked about KS2 and their outdoor play.
Data analysis date	Jan and Feb 2020.
Data analysis notes	• KS2 have less time to play outdoors other than at "playtime." • Mr Gregshaw knew it was important, he liked the idea but said other subjects tend to take up all of the timetable. • We asked if other subjects could be taught outdoors as children play. Mr G. said they could but at the moment we don't. • Mr G. knows it is important to play and be outdoors and he spoke about children's well-being and health. • He is looking forward to hearing our findings to hopefully make changes to next year's curriculum.

Figure 9.6: (*Continued*)

Analysing data

Organising the data is the first stage of analysis, but once your young researchers have done this, the real work begins! It is a good idea to begin to analyse the data as it is collected, rather than to wait until the data collection phase is complete. For example, if you are using a Likert scale (e.g. 1 = strongly agree; 2 = somewhat agree, etc.) for a questionnaire, you can keep a tally of responses for each score as you collect your questionnaires back in.

For some data analysis, researchers use categories that have already been decided, e.g. counting up the number of people who gave a particular choice of response to a multiple-choice questionnaire. Another important way of analysing data is to look carefully for themes that arise from the data – do several participants all talk about or demonstrate a similar idea (e.g. like the teachers at Cockshut Hill who all used questioning to support their modelling). Young researchers can also look for similarities and differences within and between different categories of participants (e.g. do teachers tend to have a different opinion from pupils?). Do older children and younger children have similar or different ideas? At this stage in the project, it is important to keep the young researchers' focus on the data. Data analysis is about looking for themes and patterns in the data you have collected and not about using selective bits of data to support your own opinions. Children may need reassurance at this stage that it is perfectly fine if some of your research findings are not what you might have predicted. In fact, this can be a very good thing as it means that you are shedding new light on a particular situation.

It can be very helpful for young researchers to represent their data visually, for example using pie charts or bar charts. Most children are already familiar with these methods of representing data and charts can help to show young researchers whether a particular finding is significant, as well as being useful for inclusion in your final research report.

Presenting your findings

Our young researchers all present their findings at the Young Researchers Project Conference. As discussed in Chapter 3, this involves preparing a PowerPoint presentation and/or a poster to show what the research involved and what they found out. Young researchers also present their projects to governors, senior leaders, fellow pupils and parents. Whoever you are presenting the research to and whether this is face to face or in a written report, make sure you include the following information:

- Title of the research project
- Research question/s
- Research methods
- Ethical issues
- Findings and implications of the findings
- Reflections on the research project.

Reflecting on the research project is useful for the group and for each individual researcher. Children can think about what worked well in their project and what they might do differently in a future research study. This can be used for the next group of young researchers. On an individual level, this is an opportunity for children to recognise their own personal achievements on the project e.g. have they increased confidence in speaking in front of others? Have they worked well as a member of the team? Have they improved an particular skill?

What next?

It is important for young researchers to know what will happen as a result of their research project. For example, will senior leaders use their findings when making decisions about resources or the school environment? Will their research be used to help inform the school development plan? If young researchers' projects are going to be used to open up spaces for children's voices to be heard, communicating the next steps in relation to their project is vital. You may also want to consider whether your young researchers will mentor other children in future projects, as in the case study about Taylor's pupils in Chapter 3.

The University Day presentation

We use the puzzle in Figure 9.7 at the beginning of the University Day, to engage the children and to get them thinking about their role as researchers.

In the main presentation at our University Day, we go on to discuss the following key areas with the children:

R

ES

EARC

HISLIKE

BEINGADETE

CTIVEWHOISLOOKI

NGFORCLUESANDWORKINGOU

T W H A T T H E Y M E A N

Figure 9.7: What is research?

- Research methods (including qualitative and quantitative)
- Ethics
- Literature searches and the role of university librarians and academics.

We aim to make the University Day as interactive as possible, but at the same time we do not shy away from introducing children to the ideas and vocabulary associated with carrying out 'real' research projects. So for example, we talk about ways in which you can find out the answers to your research questions and how to approach collecting data that can be quantified as opposed to data that cannot. These ideas can be demonstrated by relating them to situations that the children might have already experienced in school. So for example, we talk about choosing the right research method for the project by relating to children's understanding of choosing the best measuring tool for a mathematics task. We ask them, if you want to find out who is the tallest in the class, would you measure them using a 30 cm ruler or a non-standard unit of measure (we use a hedgehog paperweight here!)? We can then link this to a discussion of interviews, questionnaires and observations, in terms of considering which method is best for seeking out the information needed in a research project.

We then go on to consider those types of data that are less quantifiable. So, for example, if you wanted to find out who is the cheekiest person in your class, how would you do this? This leads into a discussion that covers qualitative methods as well as considering ethics. First of all, is it a good idea to research this particular question and if not, why not? What harm might be caused by this research? How would we know if our data was reliable, if it is based on opinion? And so on.

At the University Day, we also introduce ourselves as the children's research assistants and explain how they can contact us with their research questions. We remind them that any emails sent to us need to come from their school email accounts and need to follow school policy (e.g. our primary school researchers communicate with us via their teachers' email accounts so that safeguarding policies are carefully followed).

Useful sources of further support and information

1. Little Voices https://www.lleisiaubach.org/home
   This website includes information and publications used by the Little Voices project, working with children as researchers with links to Swansea and Bangor universities.
2. The Children's Research Centre at the Open University http://wels.open. ac.uk/research/childrens-research-centre
   This website includes information and resources for people working with children as researchers, based on the work of the Children's Research Centre, began by Professor Mary Kellett.
3. *Developing Children as Researchers: A Practical Guide to Help Children Conduct Social Research* (Kim et al., 2017)
   This practical book gives detailed guidance on how to approach each stage of a research project in social sciences when working with children as researchers.

References

Bucknall, S. (2012) *Children as Researchers in Primary Schools: Choice, Voice and Participation.* Routledge: Abingdon.

Kim, C., Sheehy, K. and Kerawall, L. (2017) *Developing Children as Researchers: A Practical Guide to Help Children Conduct Social Research.* Routledge: Oxon.

Chapter Ten

Young researchers in the future

Ali Fisher and Debbie Reel

Introduction

The journey of the Young Researchers Project has been one of learning and discovery for both the children taking part in active research and the teachers who have engaged with and supported children through the process. As previously described, each school has approached the research using similar tools and overall methodology, with the same guidance and access to research. However, each research focus has differed greatly, reflecting the culture and desired improvements of each school and the interests of the children. Our approach to generating research–active schools where children have a meaningful voice has been largely successful as evidenced through children's engagement and the final conference, but now needs to evolve to ensure it is future proofed. There have been a number of questions that have arisen since we first started the Young Researchers Project and the project does not stay the same every year. Einarsdottir (2007) acknowledges that children are not a homogeneous group and there is not a single method that fits all, and this can make managing the project across several schools complex.

The limitations of time

Perhaps the most frequently asked question asked by those involved is related to time. This has proved to be the biggest barrier to carrying out active research within a school setting each year. Teachers have been afforded the opportunity to engage children in the research process; however, this has not always been coupled with the time required, which has been a major challenge for those leading research from the start of the programme. Each year, teachers manage to work successfully with children despite time-related hurdles; however, we have already discussed in Chapters 1, 2 and 5 how the most successful projects are those where research is embedded into the school ethos. It is important that the Senior Leadership Team at any school embraces a culture of research and embed it as part of the school ethos, which will secure success and longevity for the Young Researchers Project and give it a high priority in the school strategy (Leat & Reid 2012).

A whole school, inclusive approach

Teachers have shown a unified willingness to support the research process and to encourage young researchers, as illustrated in our case studies in Chapters 5 to 8. Currently, however, young researchers' projects are often seen as part of 'extra-curricular' provision, however highly valued. Whilst this remains the status quo, working in this way alongside the day-to-day life of school will not embed the research process as an important aspect of whole school development. Consequently, this could undermine the overall importance placed on the research process and outcomes. We will continue to work with schools to develop a culture that truly values and celebrates the importance of pupil voice as a continual aspect of school life and not simply as an event that occurs once a year at the Young Researchers Conference.

The annual journey that the Young Researchers Project takes, including the selection of children as researchers, has been discussed in Chapters 3 and 4. Whilst the selection of participants is key, we also need to ensure that the premise of research remains inclusive and not selective. One of the successes of our project has built on the work of Clark and Moss (2011) who listened to the voices of the youngest children in order to instigate child led change. The Young Researchers Project has not shied away from encouraging the youngest participants. However, a caveat to be considered is that the children need to be able to articulate and synthesise information to actively play a part in some of our research activities. Being able to stand up in front of their peers, teachers and invited guests currently plays a part in the selection process, as the end of the research project involves each school presenting at the previously described conference. Whilst the selection of the young researchers is key, so is the aspect of inclusivity and offering all children the opportunity to participate.

As a developing project, we need to consider how the concept of a child as a researcher is constructed and how we choose to analyse this in making decisions as to who engages in the process, as suggested by Janzen (2008). There is the potential to develop different modes of carrying out and disseminating research, so that children with Special Educational Needs might be more involved in the projects, for example.

Research assistants have provided support in the presentation of the final projects at the Young Researchers Conference. Each year there is a discussion between adults involved in the project around how best to present findings. There have been a variety of formats; presentations, poster presentations with discussions and a mixture of the two. This debate is fruitful and ongoing as we do not want to lose the voice of the child. As stated by Kellett (2009, p. 242) 'The further a child's voice strays from the articulate, performative ideal that is prized in adult forums, the fainter it becomes'. We need to ensure that the child's voice remains prominent and that we continue to develop ways in which less articulate children can be involved in carrying out and presenting their research.

A whole class approach

The case studies have illustrated differing approaches to the selection of participating pupils. Schools have held ballots and asked children to apply with a vote to decide who should represent their school. Other schools have selected children from differentiated groups such as gifted and talented or pupils with challenging behaviour. Perhaps the greatest hurdle to jump in relation to who participates in the Young Researchers Project concerns the limitation placed on numbers and the manageability of group sizes. Whilst the project currently offers the opportunity for only six to eight children from each school to participate, it will remain primarily an exclusive programme. Research by children already faces several levels of critique that have been discussed in Chapter 3; we need to ensure that exclusivity does not become another in our projects. Tara has shown in Chapter 6 that it is possible to involve the whole class in a research project and this is something that we intend to develop further as the Young Researchers Project evolves.

Involving a whole class in the research process promotes the importance of children as researchers. The value of this research being embedded in the whole school ethos has potential for a greater impact for all children in all schools. We will now trial teachers working with all of their children across the year giving the class the opportunity to present to peers, teachers, parents and governors. Having had the experience of presenting 'in house', there could then be a representative group of children who present findings at the annual conference. Working on a broader scale with a wider range of children may well create additional hurdles that will have to be negotiated, but will also provide some impactful and meaningful data for whole school development.

Wider research questions

With researchers decided upon, the choosing of a research question has raised many questions each year and has been another challenging aspect of the whole process. A key source of support has been the link between school and university and their respective expertise and access to research. The University Day, as previously discussed, has proven to be an invaluable start to the process. Schools have used the lecturers' expertise to pose questions, confirm thinking and to better shape research questions through their knowledge of the topic explored. As a starting point, schools have been guided towards their School Improvement Plan (SIP) to find inspiration for the research question whilst others have been guided by the headteacher. Murray (2016) acknowledges the value children as researchers can add to policy and curriculum development.

Choice of the research area is key. Schools have been encouraged to ensure meaningful questions are devised and that the research is not influenced by a topic where the answer is already known. The wording of the question, once the research area had been decided, has also proved a challenge and one that was regularly discussed during half-termly meetings where questions were shared, discussed and reframed. Although this initially presented as a challenge, teachers did develop in their understanding of the value of research and the impact on their class. As the project develops, we can encourage children and teachers to move beyond their own classrooms to research questions that impact more widely on the community as a whole.

The potential for extending the Young Researchers Project and its philosophy is endless. There are many opportunities to look outside of the school and have an influence in the local or wider community. As a key stakeholder in a school, having a positive impact on the environment beyond the school gates within the community is both enriching and empowering. As discussed in Chapter 3, this project has the opportunity to create more of a social pedagogical approach to research carried out by young children as they have the opportunity to research and reshape the fundamentals of their local and wider community where the shared activity extends beyond school and better represents the place in which children live. This gives a social pedagogical element to the research as children play a wider role in society. This may include collaboration with other schools, including international schools or the private sector.

Measuring impact

It is the value of the whole process that has caused the next issue for debate. The measurement of impact on the children and indeed teachers involved in the programme presents an ongoing challenge. Evaluation of the project at the end of the year takes the form of an evaluation sheet for both children and teachers. Children grow in confidence during the duration of the programme and non-cognitive outcomes such as team work, communication skills and aspiration are recorded. As discussed in Chapter 6, Leat and Reid (2012) make reference to a range of non-cognitive benefits that emerge from young children engaging in the research process. As the project develops, we would like to explore ways of recording a more precise picture of the impact of the project in terms of non-cognitive benefits.

We are also keen to determine whether the engagement as a researcher has an impact on academic progress, or indeed whether this is something we even need to measure. Janzen (2008) refers to children, who engage in research as 'constructors of knowledge'. Do we then assume that in constructing knowledge, academic attainment will follow? It is an aim during the next phase of this project to explore this issue; to better measure and report on outcomes for children and for staff, who may progress in leadership development as a result. Once an effective outcome measurement process is in place, future research can be seen as value added to the educational and professional journeys of both children and staff.

As we said at the beginning of the book, the Young Researchers Project is not 'finished' but something that we look forward to developing further in the years ahead.

References

Clark, A. & Moss, P. (2011) *Listening to Young Children: The Mosaic Approach*, 2nd edition. NCB: London.

Einarsdottir, J. (2007) Research with children: methodological and ethical challenges. *European Early Childhood Education Research Journal* Vol. 52, no. 1, pp. 197–211.

Janzen, M. (2008) Where is the (postmodern) child in early childhood education research? *Early Years* Vol. 28, no. 3, pp. 287–298.

Kellett, M. (2009) Children and young people's voices. In: Montgomery, H. & Kellett, M. (eds.), *Children and Young People's Worlds: Developing Frameworks for Integrated Practice*. Policy Press: Bristol.

Leat, D. & Reid, A. (2012) Exploring the role of student researchers in the process of curriculum development. *Curriculum Journal* Vol. 23, no. 2, pp. 189–205.

Murray, J. (2016) Young children are researchers: children aged four to eight years engage in important research behaviour when they base decisions on evidence. *European Early Childhood Education Research Journal* Vol. 24, no. 5, pp. 705–720.

Index

Page numbers in *italics* refer to content in *figures*; page numbers in **bold** refer to content in **tables**.